This book is to be returned on or before
the last date stamped below.

D1422901

AME

ILLUSI

SEVE

RICAN

RATION

NTEEN

Creative Direction and Design: LLOYD ZIFF • Assistant Art Director: CHRIS TEOH • Jacket Illustration: MICK HAGGERTY • End Paper Illustration: LOU BEACH • Title pages: wood typography: ROSS MACDONALD • Jury Portraits: NICHOLAS BLECHMAN by ROBERT GROSSMAN; GERALDINE HESSLER by BROOK MEINHARDT; MARK MICHAELSON by PHILIP BURKE; HOWARD REEVES by GREEN & READ; KEN SMITH by ANITA KUNZ • Index page Illustration: BOB ZOELL • Chairman: FRED WOODWARD • Publisher: KENNETH FADNER • Director: MARK HEFLIN • Jacket Copy: PEGGY ROALF • Special thanks to PARSONS SCHOOL of DESIGN for providing the space and equipment for the AMERICAN ILLUSTRATION 17 judging. • Captions and artwork in this book have been supplied by the entrants. While every effort has been made to ensure accuracy, AMERICAN ILLUSTRATION does not under any circumstances accept any responsibility for errors or omissions. • The illustrations in this book were originally published in consumer, trade and technical magazines, periodicals, newspapers and their supplements. Others were created for advertisements, promotional design, annual reports, books, cd covers, catalogs, direct mail, self-promotion, or were personal works. • AMERICAN ILLUSTRATION 17 is indexed (with addresses and telephone numbers) by illustrator including all creative personnel who took part in the creation and utilization of the illustrations in this book. • If you are a practicing illustrator, rep., someone who commissions illustration or a student and would like to submit work to the next annual competition or would like additional copies or back issues write or call to: AMERICAN ILLUSTRATION, 28 West 25th Street, 11 Floor, New York, NY 10010. Telephone: 212-243-5262 Fax: 212-243-5201 • Distributor to the United States and Canada: D.A.P./DISTRIBUTED ART PUBLISHERS, 155 Avenue of the Americas, 2nd floor, New York, NY 10013. Telephone: 212-627-1999 Fax 212-627-9484 • ISBN 1-886212-10-4 • Distributor to the Rest of the World: HEARST BOOKS INTERNATIONAL, 1350 Avenue of the Americas, New York, NY 10019. Telephone: 212-261-6770 Fax: 212-261-6795 • Printer: DAI NIPPON, Hong Kong.
• Copyright © 1998 Amilus, Inc. • All rights reserved. No part of this publication may be reproduced, stored in a retrieval system, or transmitted in any form or any means, electronic, mechanical, photocopying, recording or otherwise, without prior permission of the copyright owners.

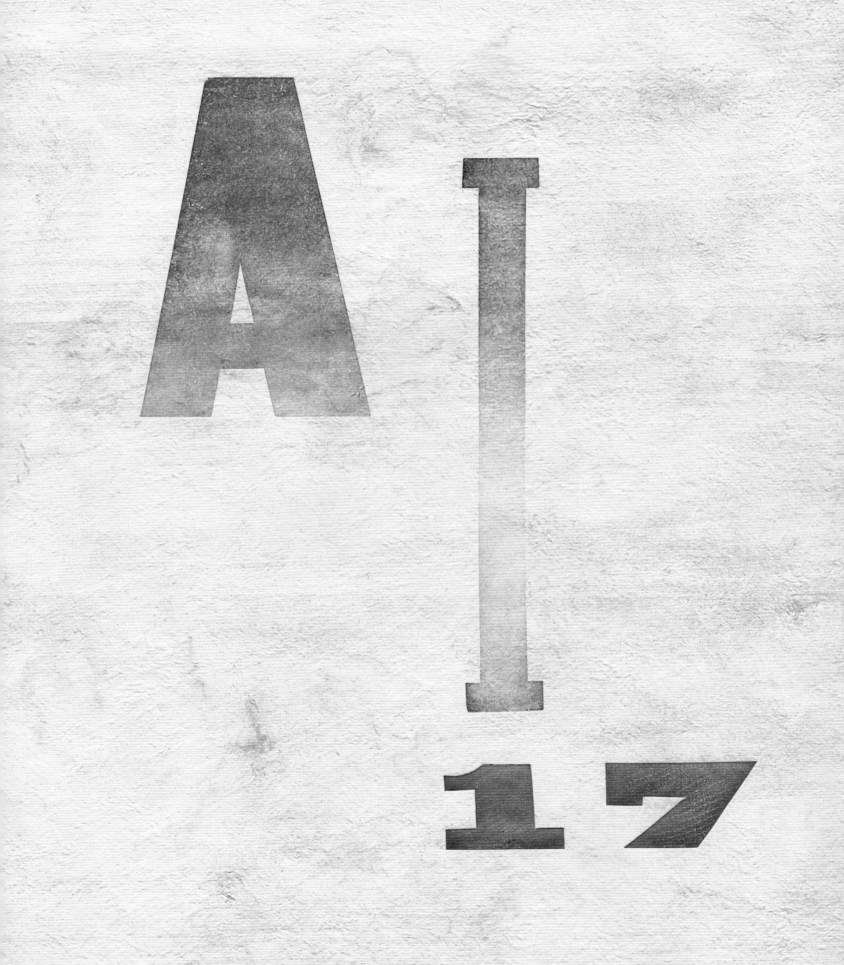

The Jury

GERALDINE HESSLER
Art Director
ENTERTAINMENT WEEKLY

•

illustrated by
BROOK MEINHARDT

NICHOLAS BLECHMAN
Art Director
THE NEW YORK TIMES OP-ED

•

illustrated by
ROBERT GROSSMAN

MARK MICHAELSON
Design Director
NEW YORK MAGAZINE

•

illustrated by
PHILIP BURKE

CITY COLLEGE
MANCHESTER
ARDEN LEARNING
RESOURCES CENTRE
061 957 1725
741.6 AME
00050231
P18761 21.1.02 £39.95

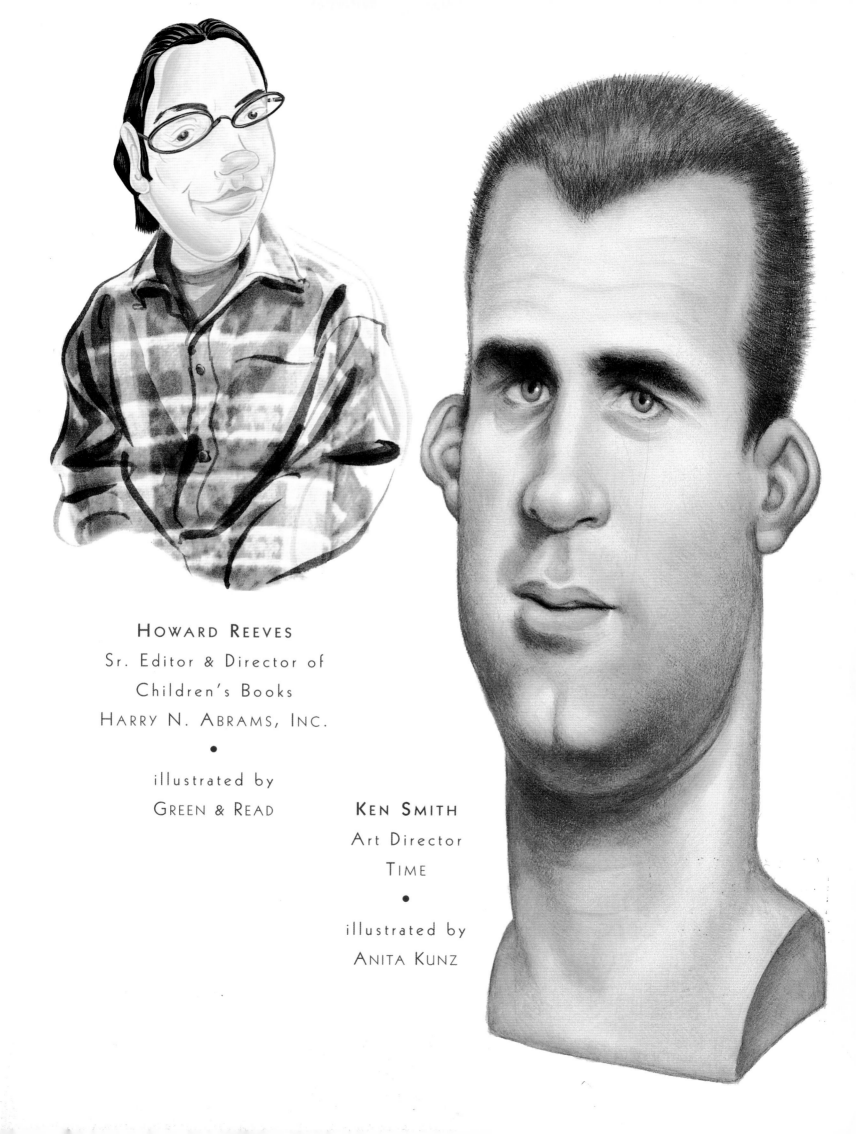

HOWARD REEVES
Sr. Editor & Director of
Children's Books
HARRY N. ABRAMS, INC.

•

illustrated by
GREEN & READ

KEN SMITH
Art Director
TIME

•

illustrated by
ANITA KUNZ

MICK AARESTRUP

DANIEL ADEL

DOUG AITKEN

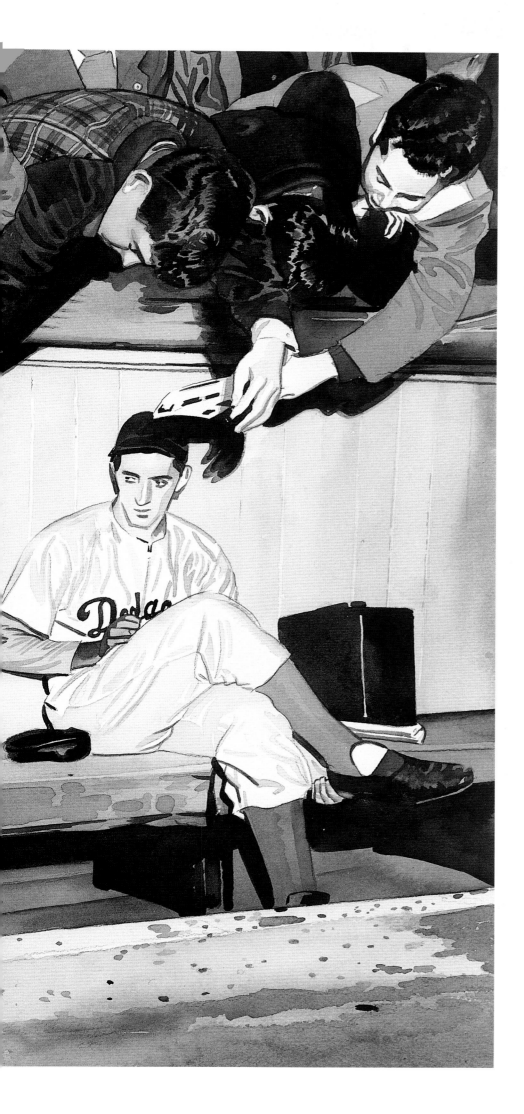

JULIAN ALLEN

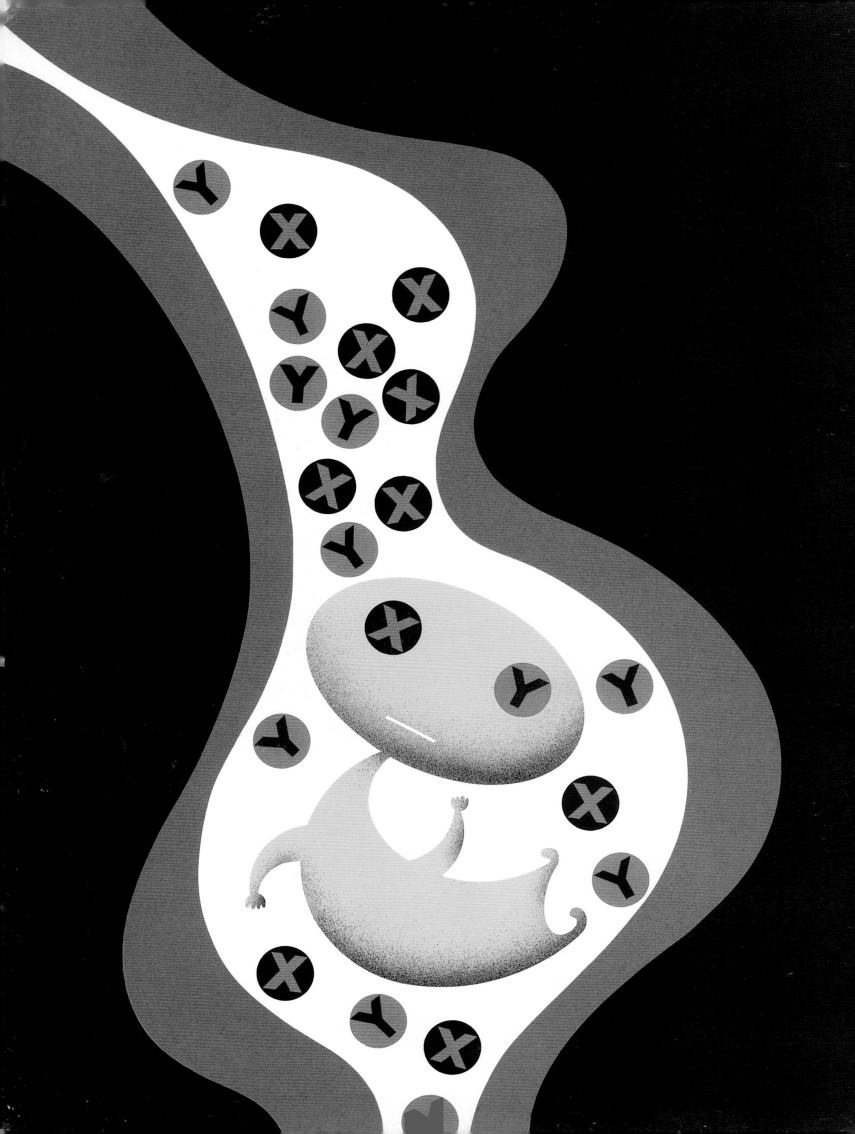

TERRY ALLEN

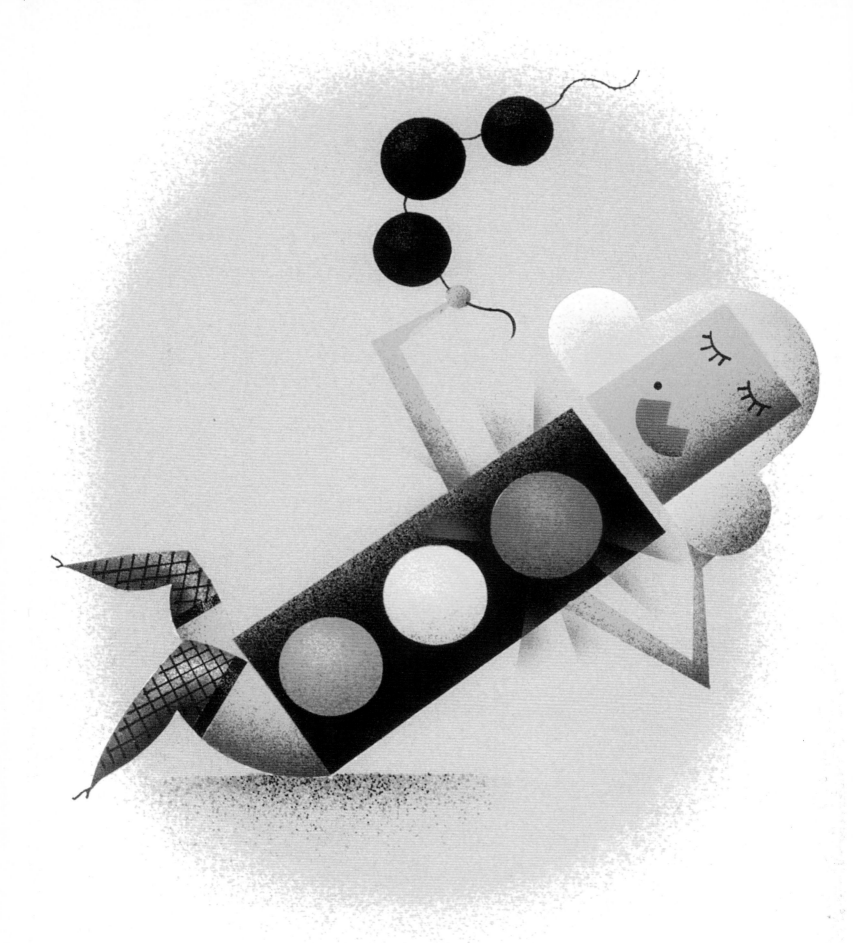

TERRY ALLEN

CHARLES S. ANDERSON

CARLOS APONTE

PATRICK ARRASMITH

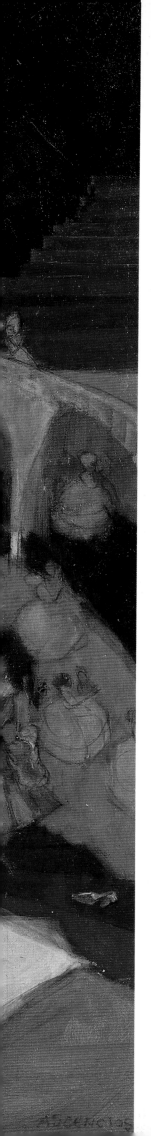

N. ASCENCIOS

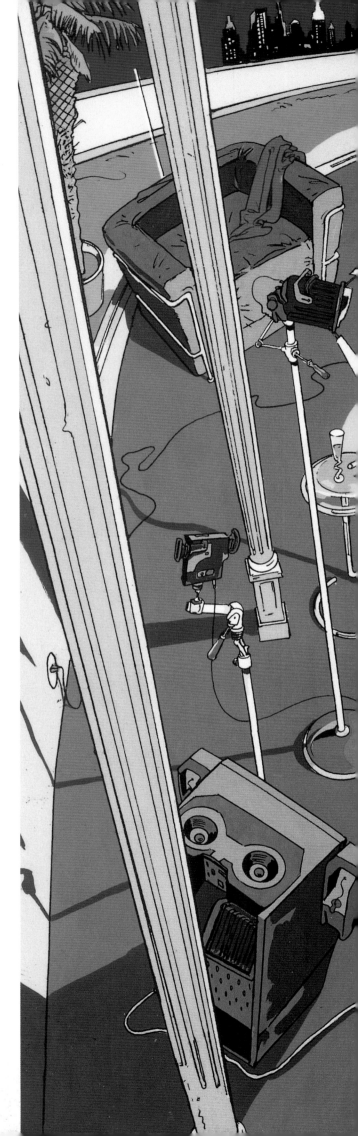

ISTVAN BANYAI

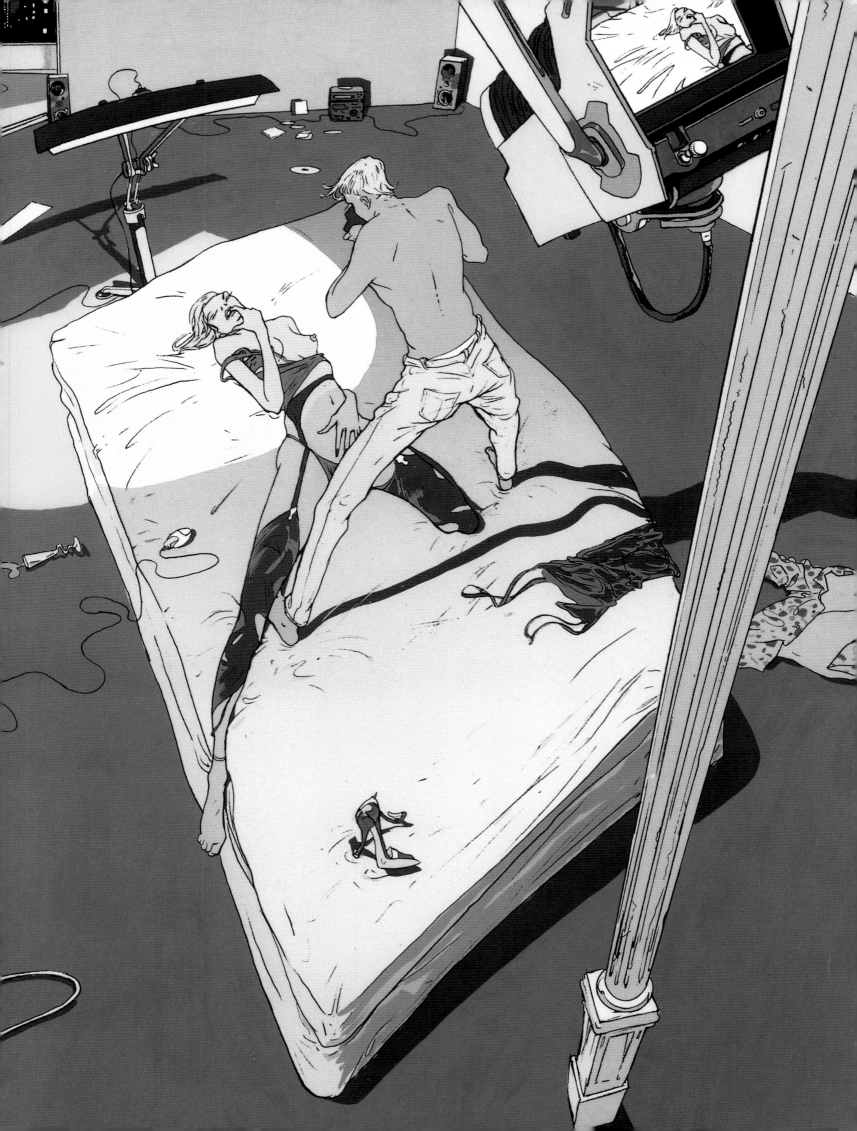

KAREN BARBOUR

DEBORAH BARRETT

GARY
BASEMAN

MELINDA BECK

WESLEY BEDROSIAN

POLLY BECKER

BENOÎT

GUY BILLOUT

RO **BLECHMAN**

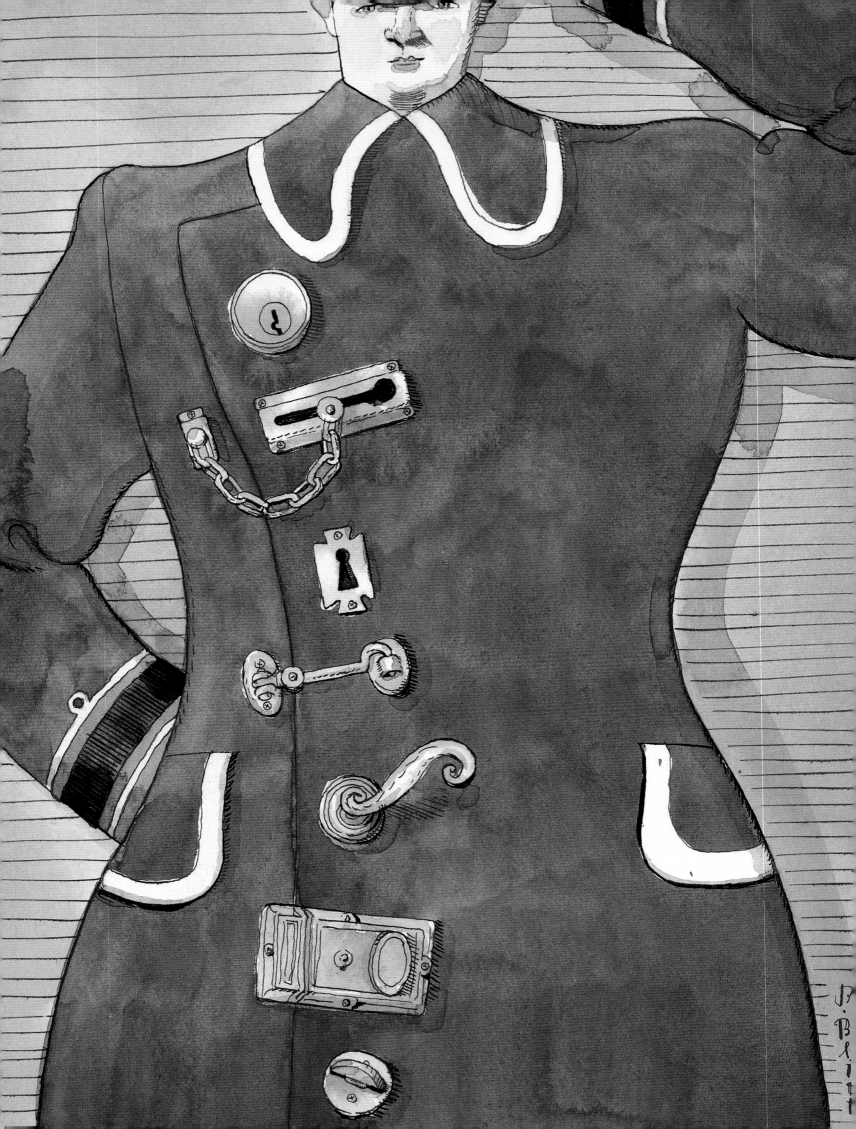

BARRY BLITT

JULIETTE BORDA

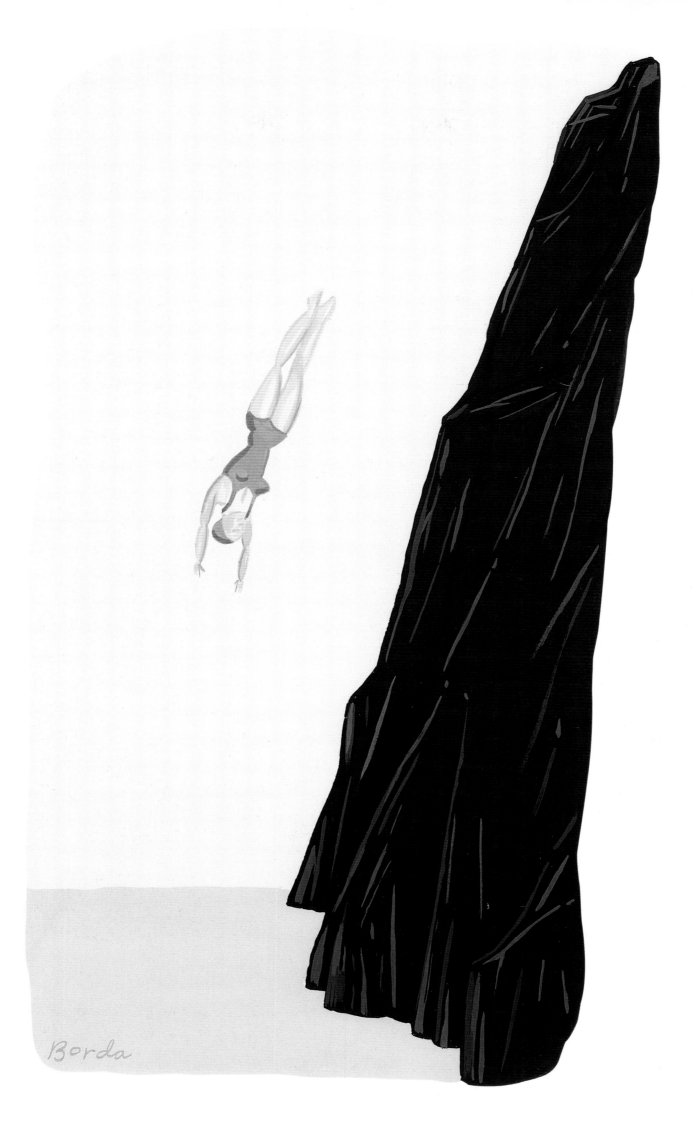

Borda

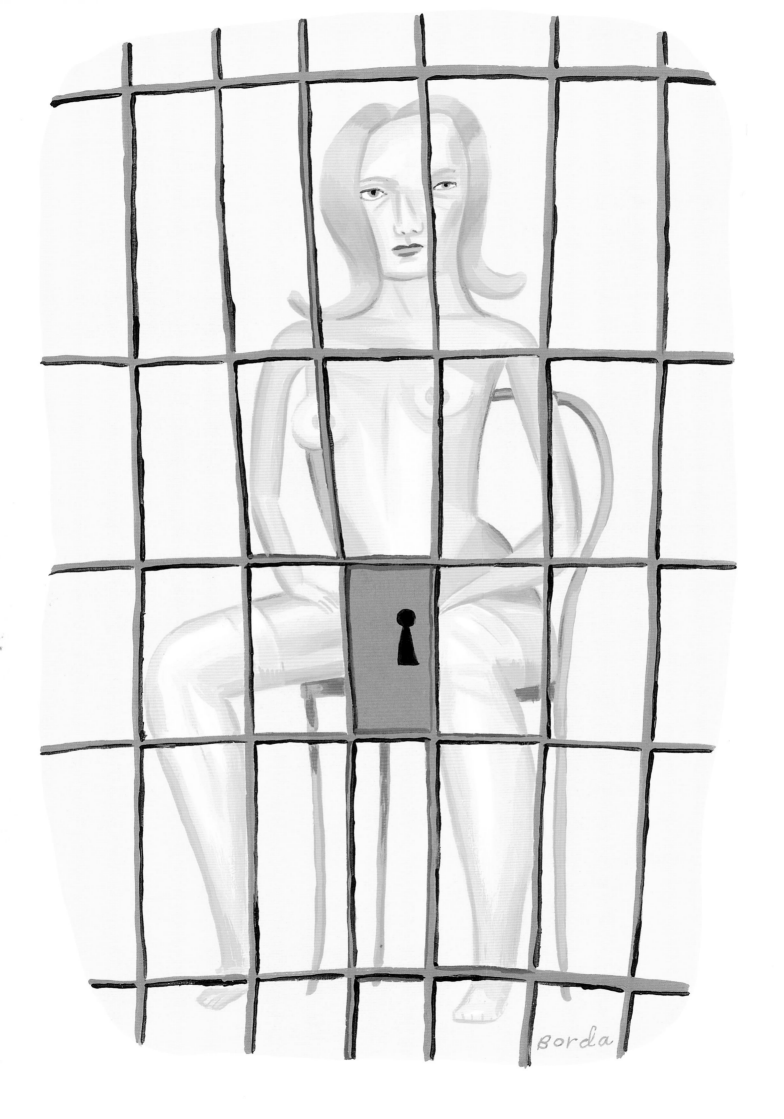

JULIETTE BORDA

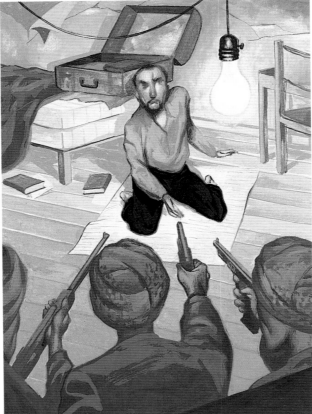

TIM BOWER

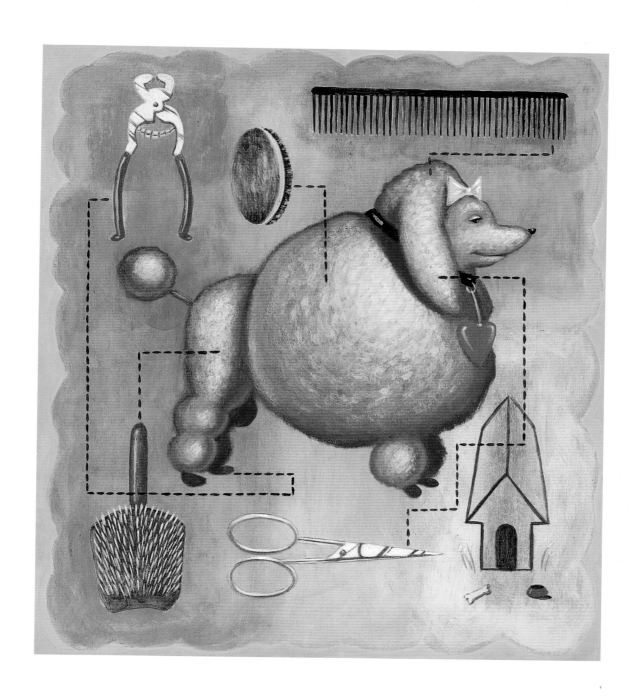

DAVID M. BRINLEY

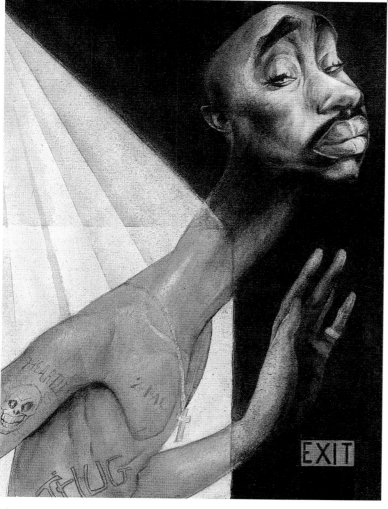

S T E V E BRODNER

STEVE **BRODNER**

CALEF BROWN

ALLAN M. BURCH

PHILIP BURKE

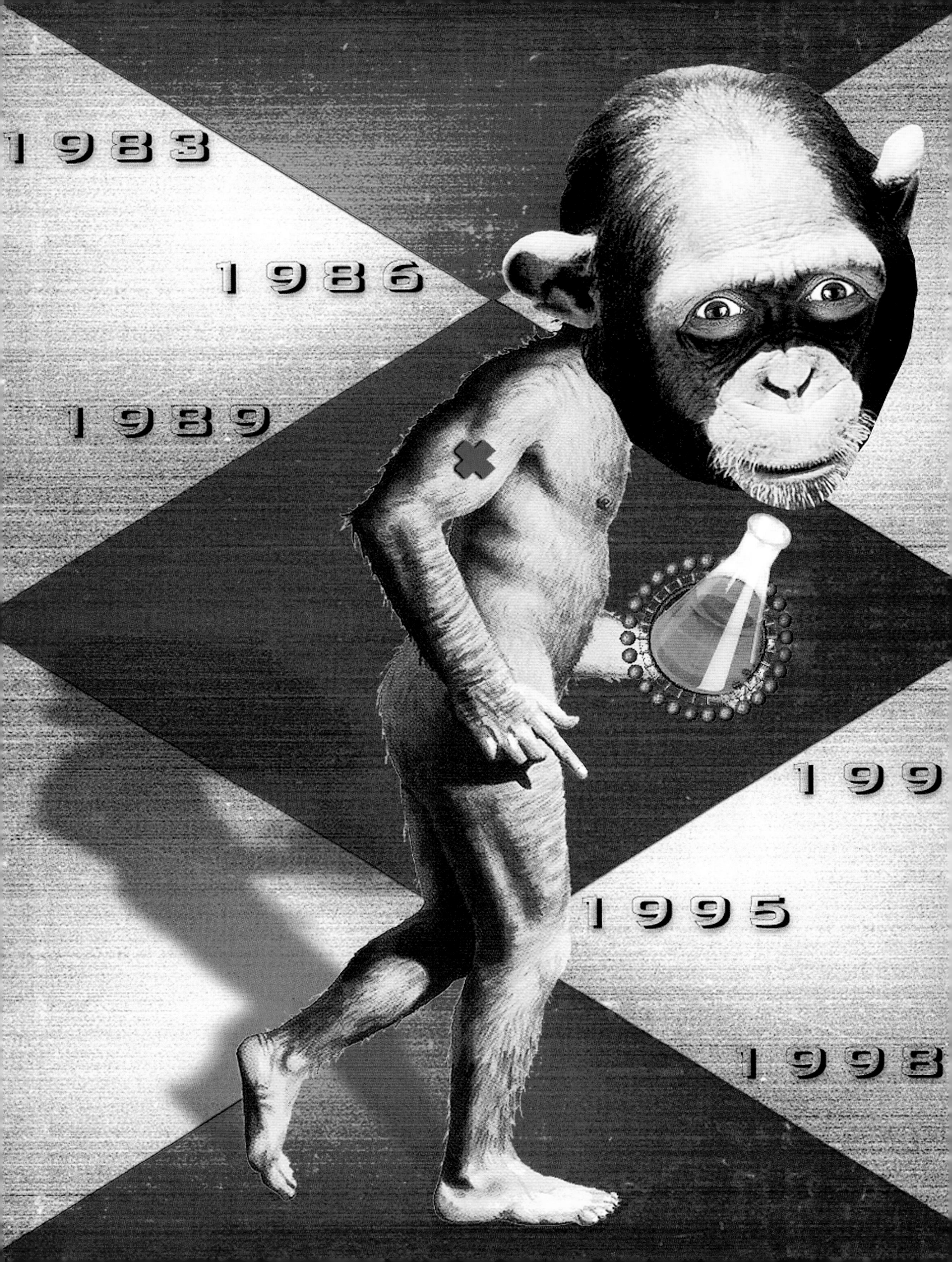
1983
1986
1989
199
1995
1998

CHRISTOPHER CANNON

FRANCISCO CACERES

MICHELLE CHANG

MICHELLE CHANG

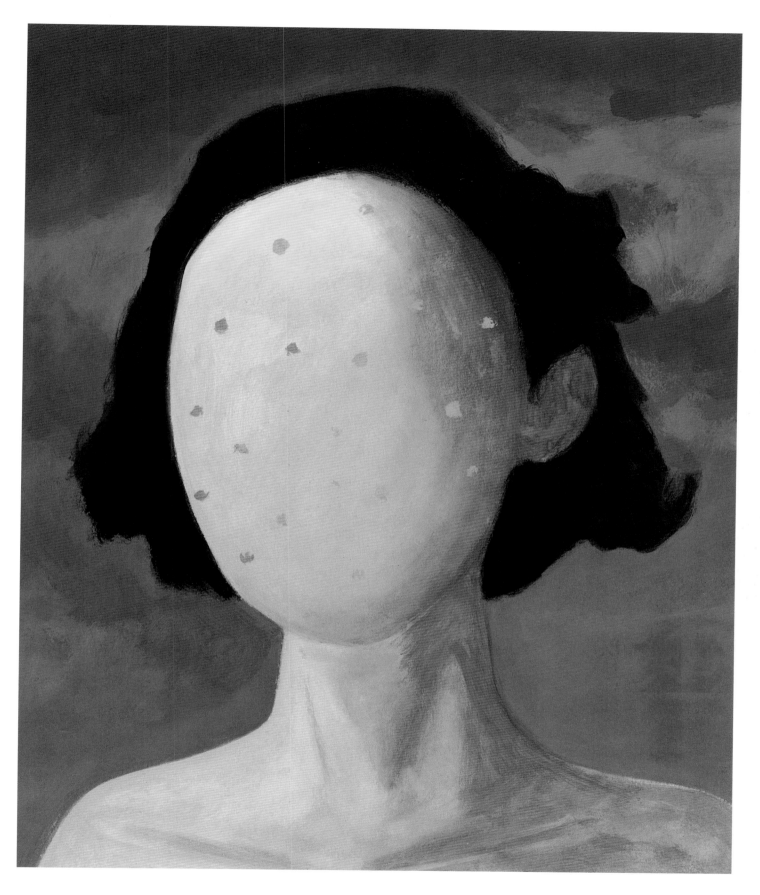

R . G R E G O R Y CHRISTIE

SEYMOUR CHWAST

GREG CLARKE

CHRISTIAN CLAYTON

CHRISTIAN CLAYTON

CHRISTIAN & ROB CLAYTON

SEASONS GREETINGS From FRIEDA & ROB CLAYTON

ROB CLAYTON

ROB CLAYTON

GARY CLEMENT

GARY CLEMENT

ALAN E. COBER

Alain E Cober

TAVIS COBURN

SUE COE

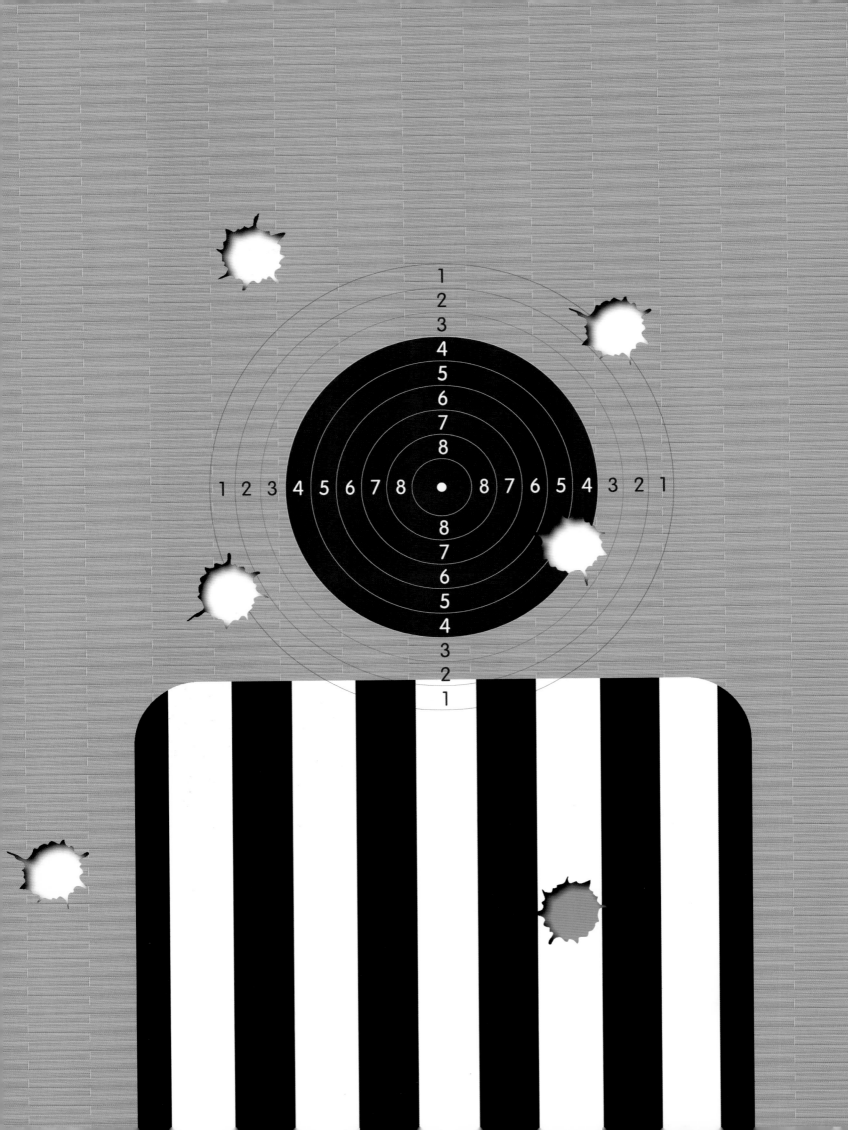

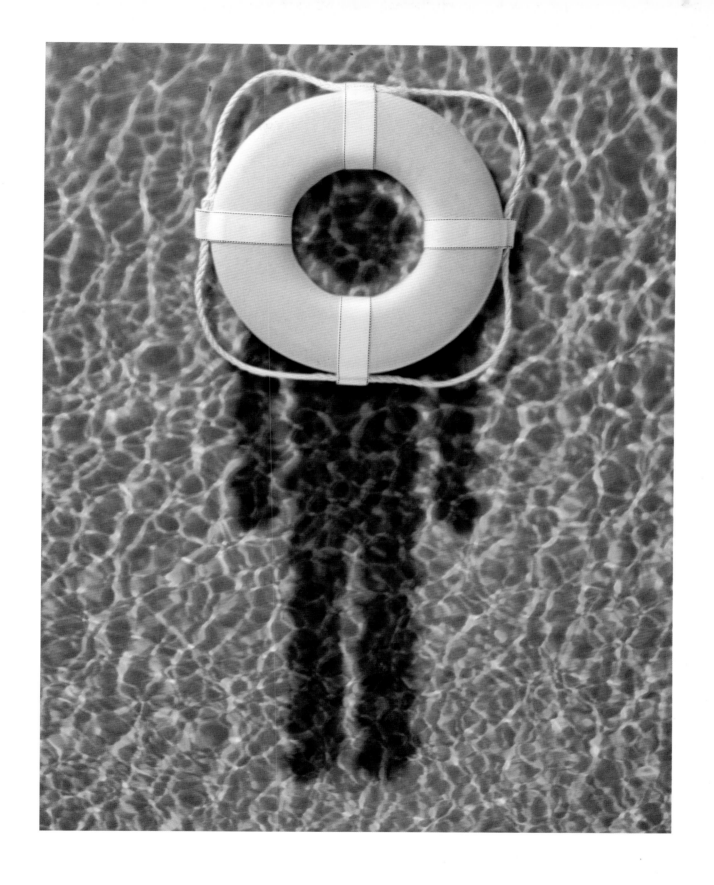

JIM COHEN

JOHN COLLIER

SANTIAGO COHEN

GENEVIÈVE CÔTÉ

BRIAN CRONIN

BRIAN CRONIN

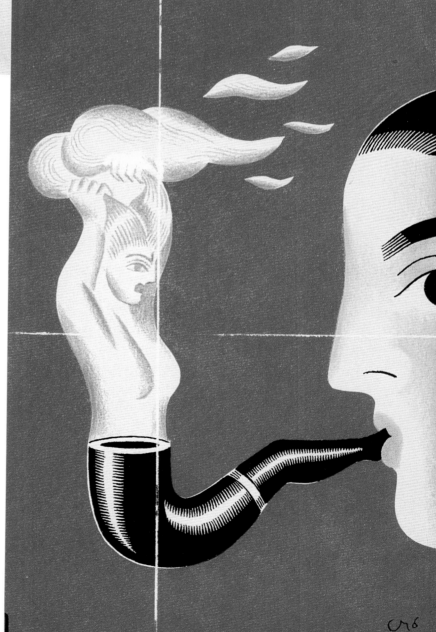

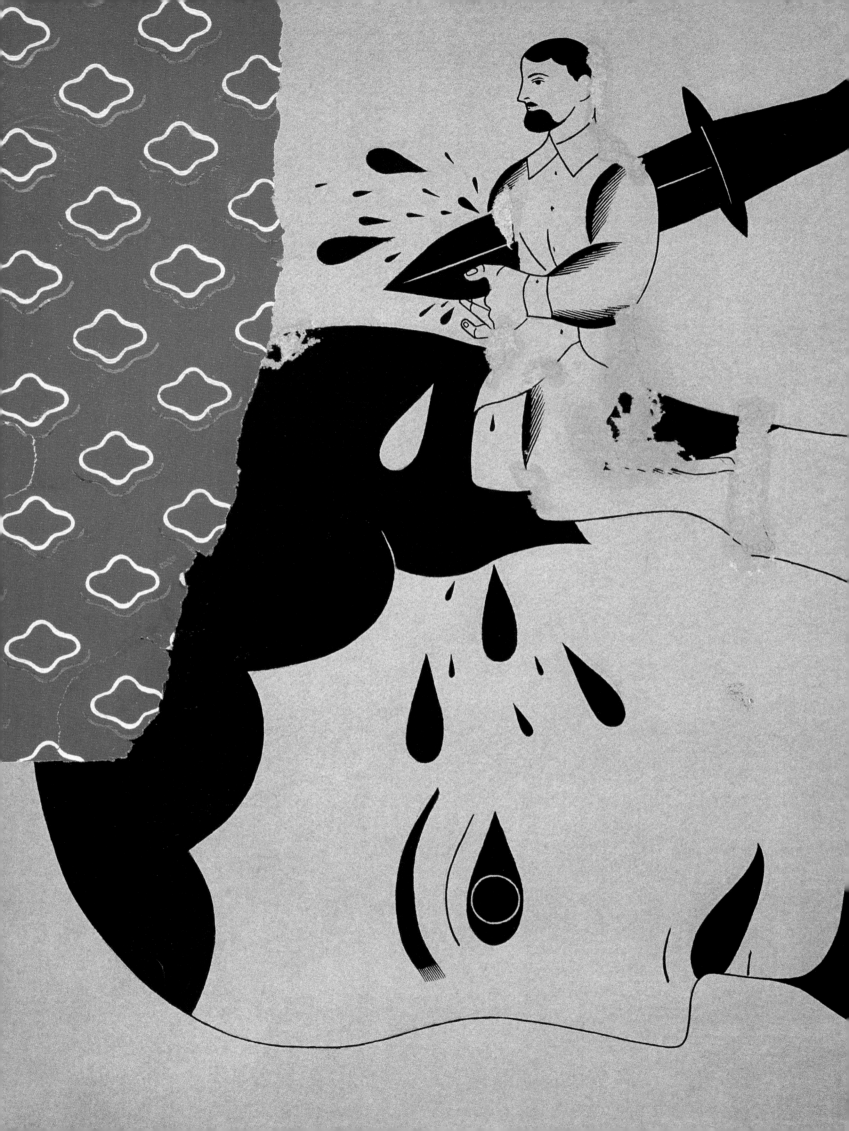

EBB
EBONY
EYE EAR EAST

BRIAN CRONIN

TODD PIPER HAUSWIRTH &
ERIK EMMINGS

ERIK T. JOHNSON

a high-paid
professional
with a high
PAIN
TRRESHOLD

PAUL DALLAS

MARK DANIELSON

PAUL DAVIS

PETER De SÈVE

PETER DE SÈVE

JEFFREY DECOSTER

KIM DEMARCO

ETIENNE DELESSERT

ISABELLE DERVAUX

NICK DEWAR

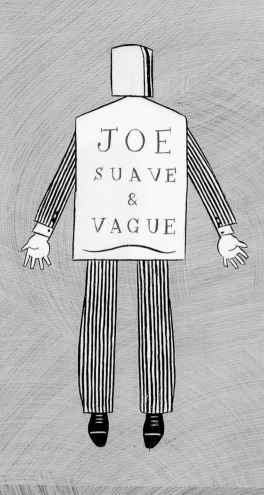

JOE
SUAVE
&
VAGUE

Jill
Sassy
& Smart

babs

cute
but
ditzy

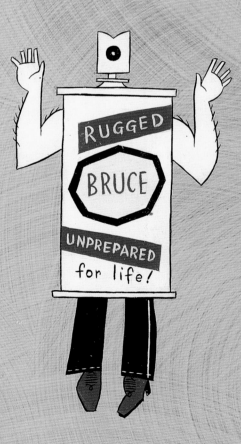

RUGGED

BRUCE

UNPREPARED

for life!

NICK DEWAR

HENRIK DRESCHER

GÉRARD DuBOIS

GÉRARD DuBOIS

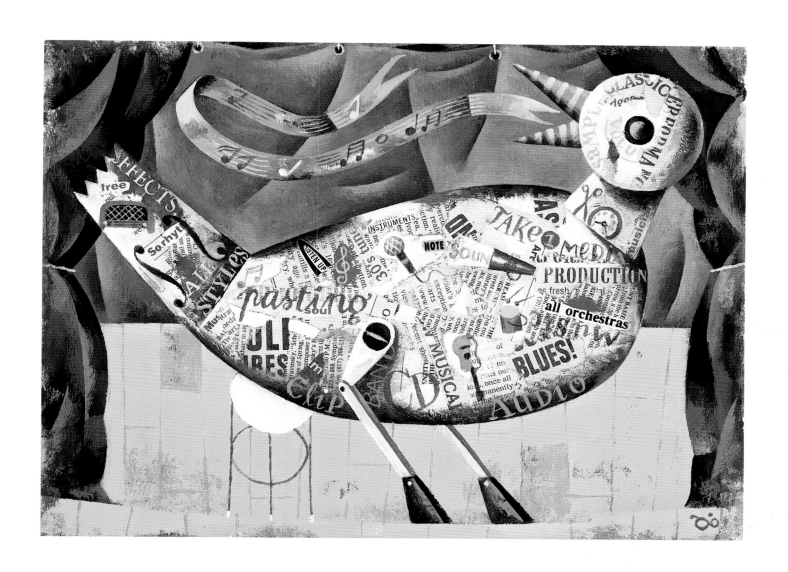

GÉRARD DuBOIS

THE DYNAMIC DUO STUDIO

IAN FALCONER

EDEM ELESH

INGO FAST

IVETTA FEDOROVA

INGO FAST

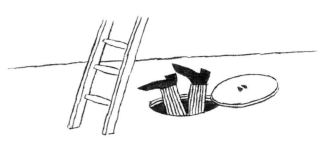

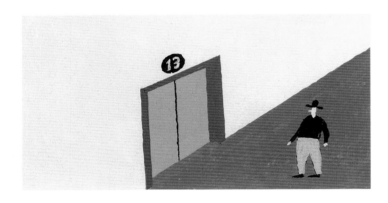

JEFFREY FISHER

VIVIENNE FLESHER

EDWIN FOTHERINGHAM

LISA FRANKE

CRAIG FRAZIER

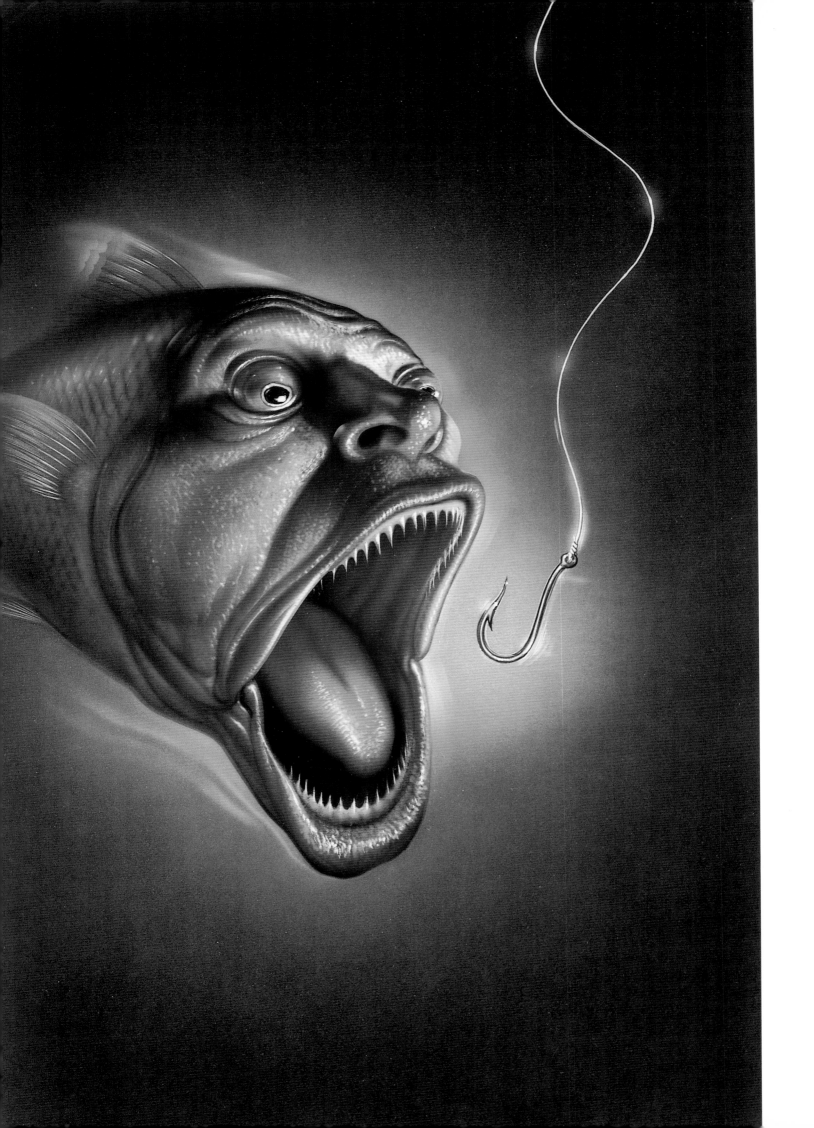

DREW
FRIEDMAN

THOMAS **FUCHS**

THOMAS FUCHS

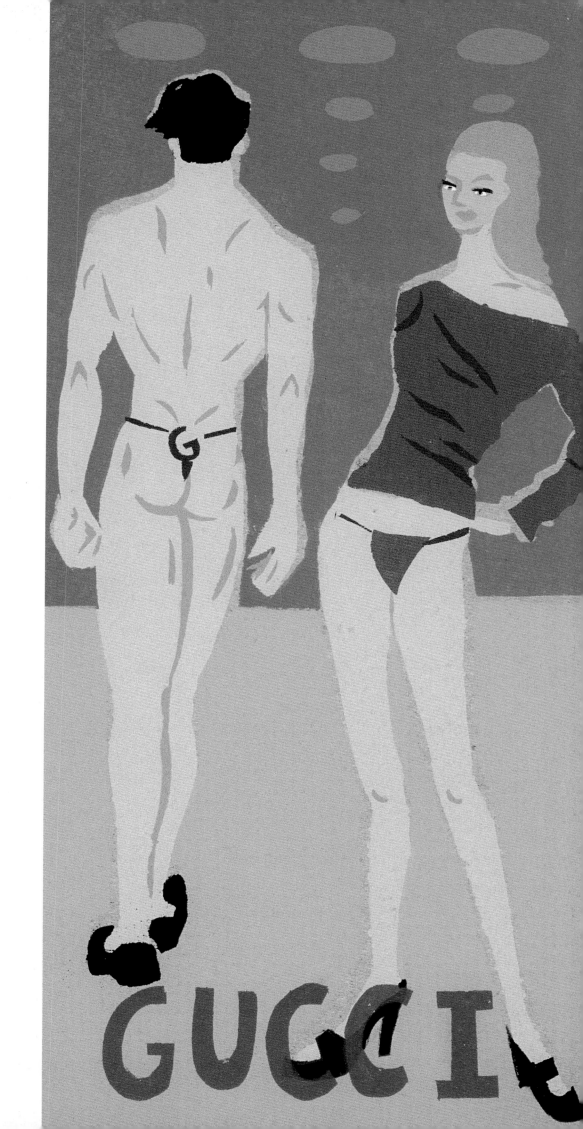

MARK GAGNON

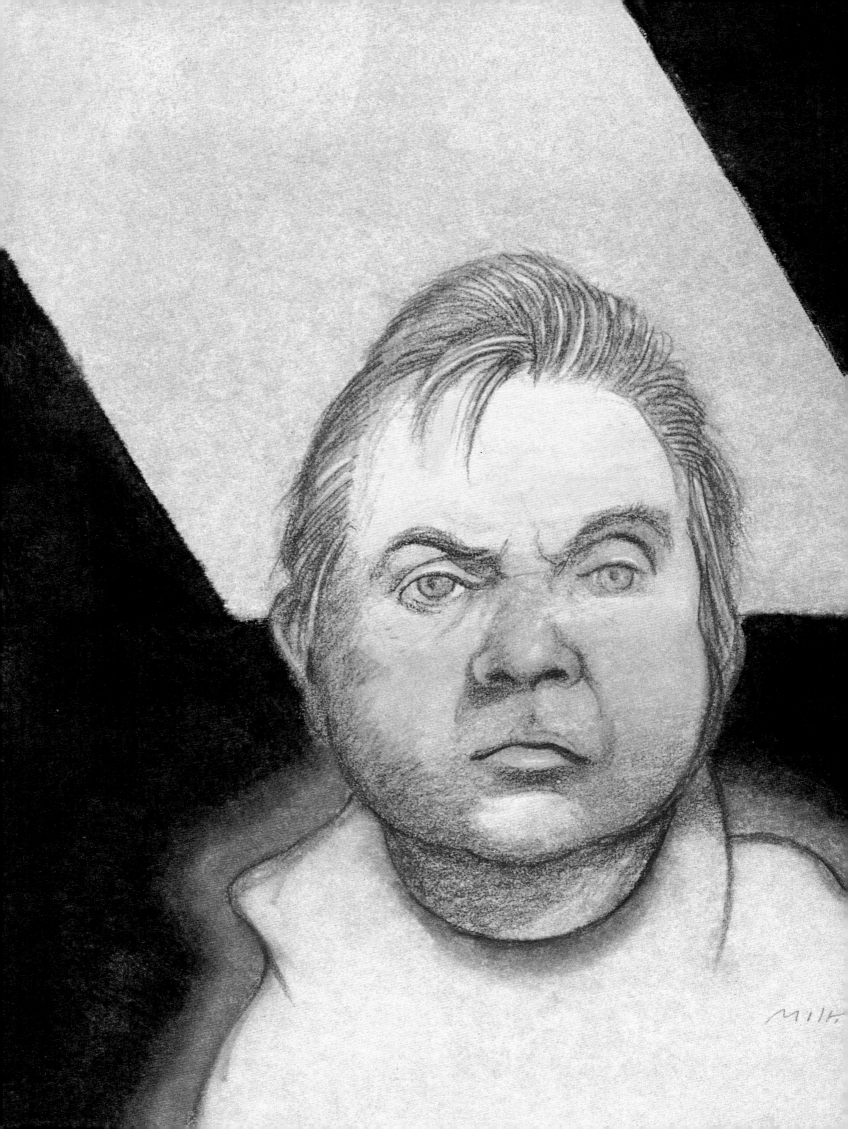

MILTON GLASER

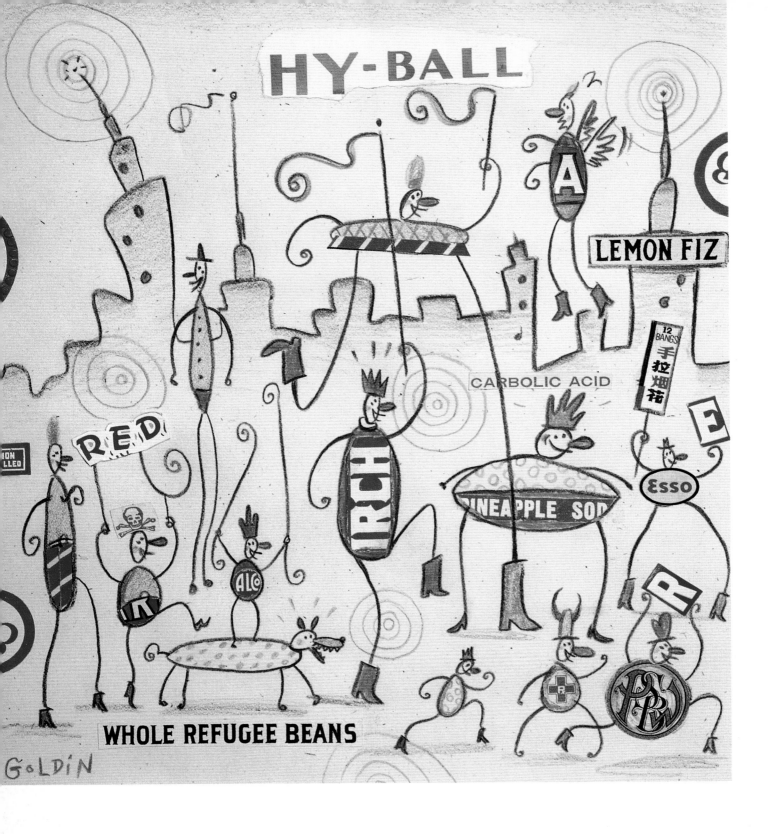

DAVID GOLDIN

EDWARD GOREY

JOSH GOSFIELD

"GOD MUST BE A LITTLE UPSET WITH HIS CREATION THAT WE CANT GET ALONG TOGETHER"

BETTY SHABAZZ

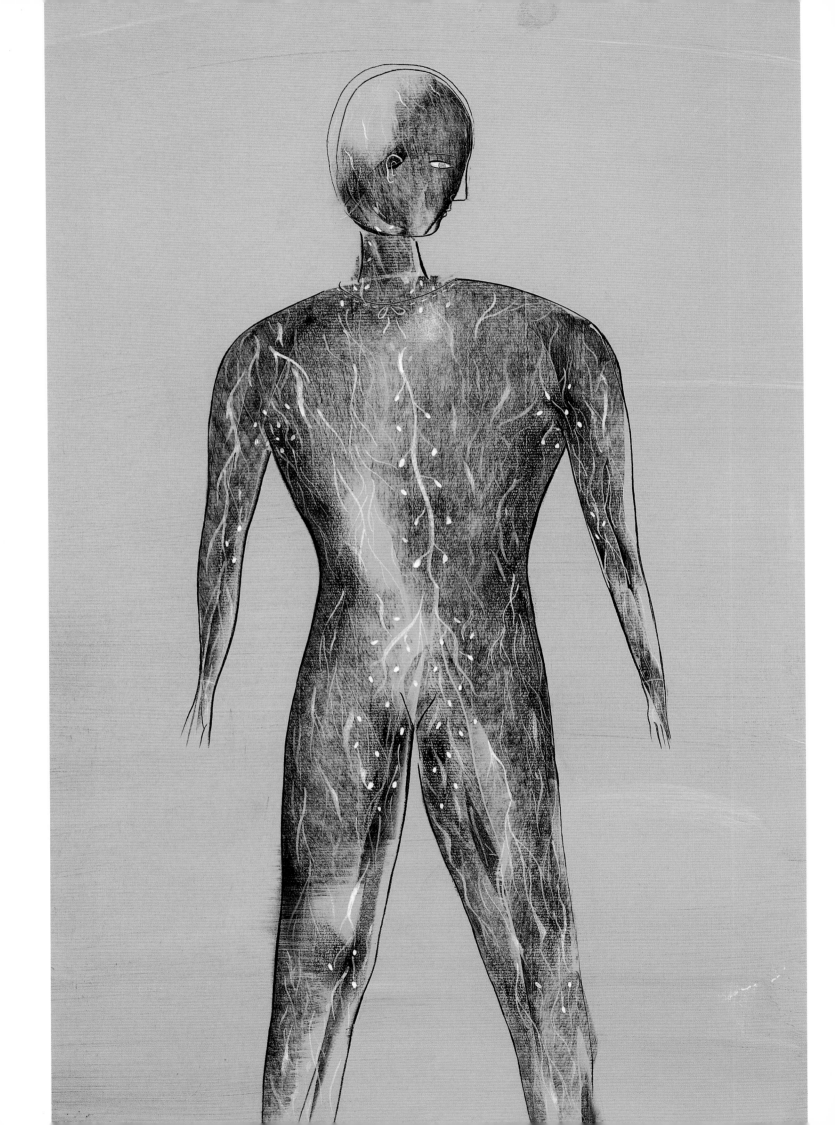

ALEXA GRACE

GEOFFREY GRAHN

GEOFFREY GRAHN

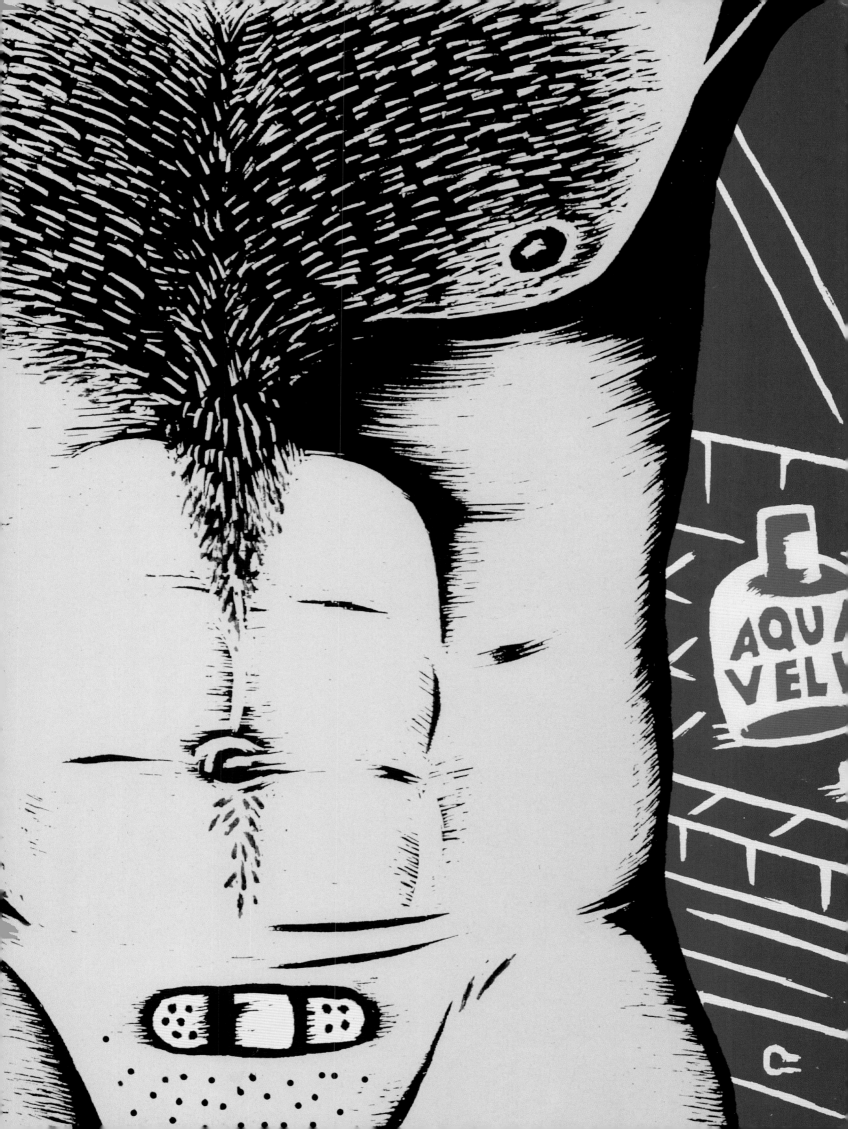

GEOFFREY GRAHN

GREEN
& READ

WILLIAM GRIFFITHS

S T E V E N GUARNACCIA

S T E V E N
GUARNACCIA

AMY GUIP

EDMUND GUY

EDMUND GUY

ERIC HANSON

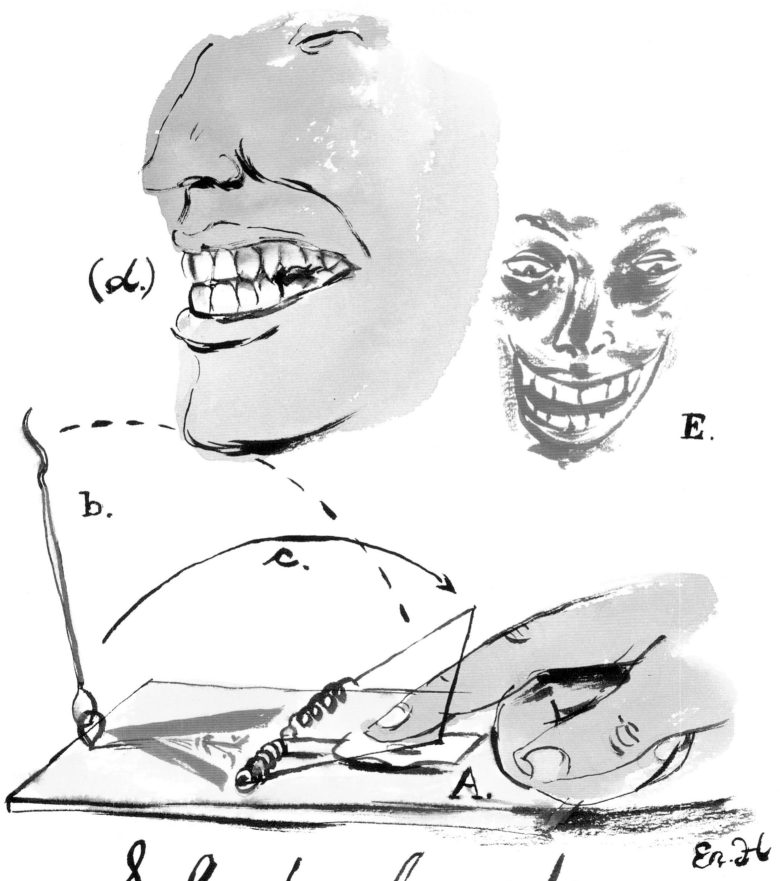

Schadenfreude

JESSIE HARTLAND

VIRGINIA HATLEY

MARTYN HEILIG

SANDRA HENDLER

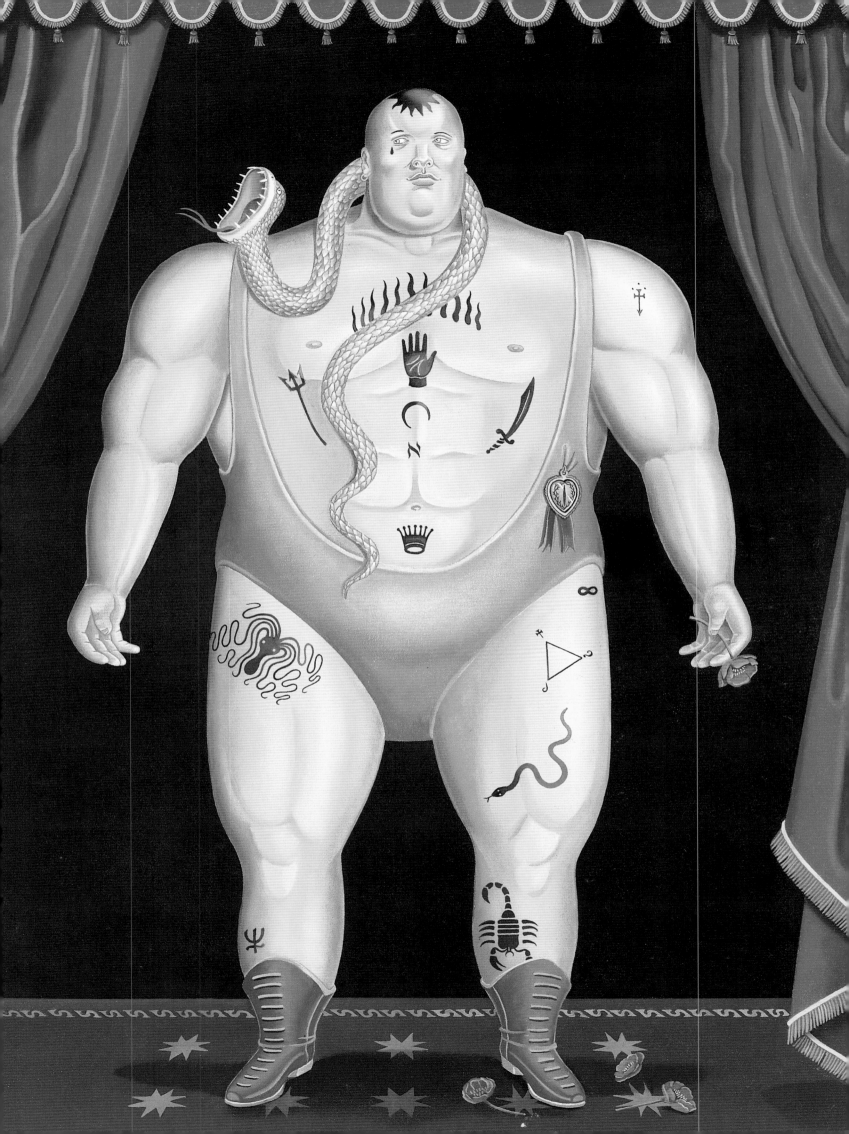

JODY HEWGILL

JOYCE HESSELBERTH

AL HIRSCHFELD

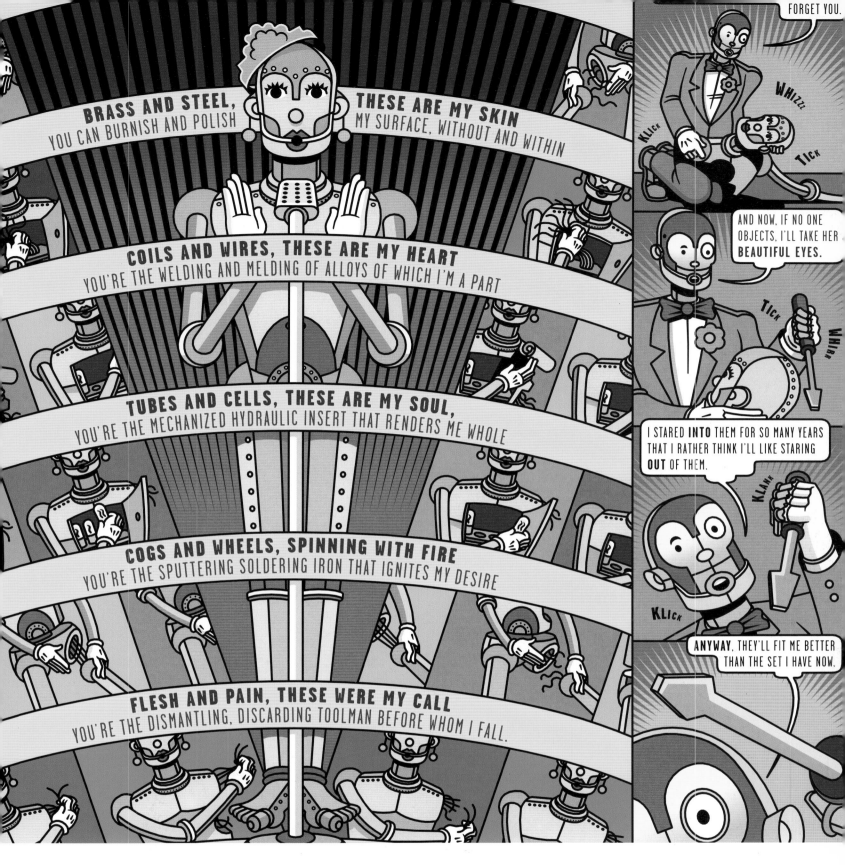

PETER HOEY

PAMELA HOBBS

BRAD HOLLAND

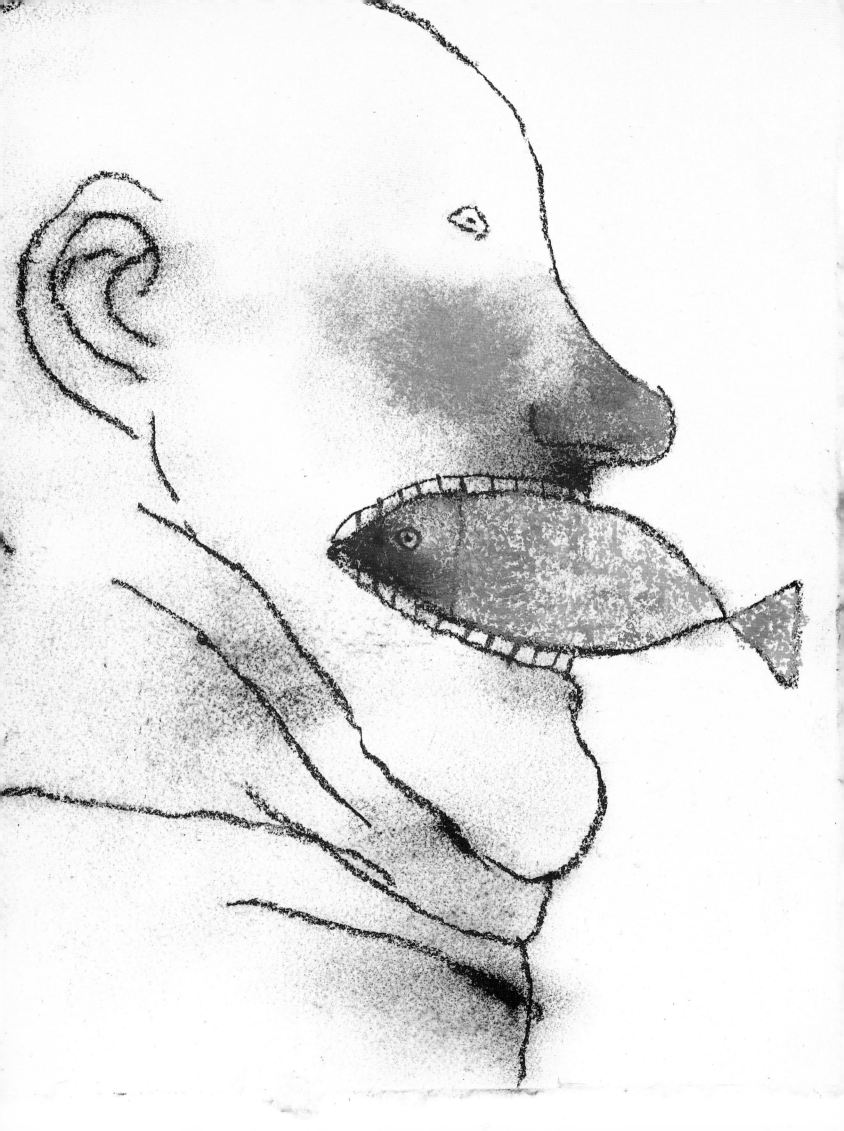

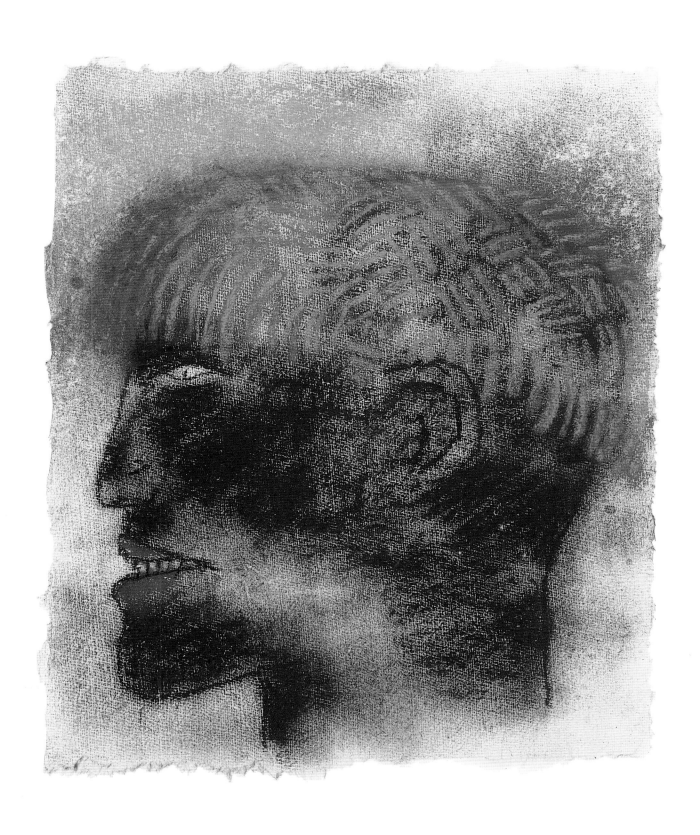

BRAD **HOLLAND**

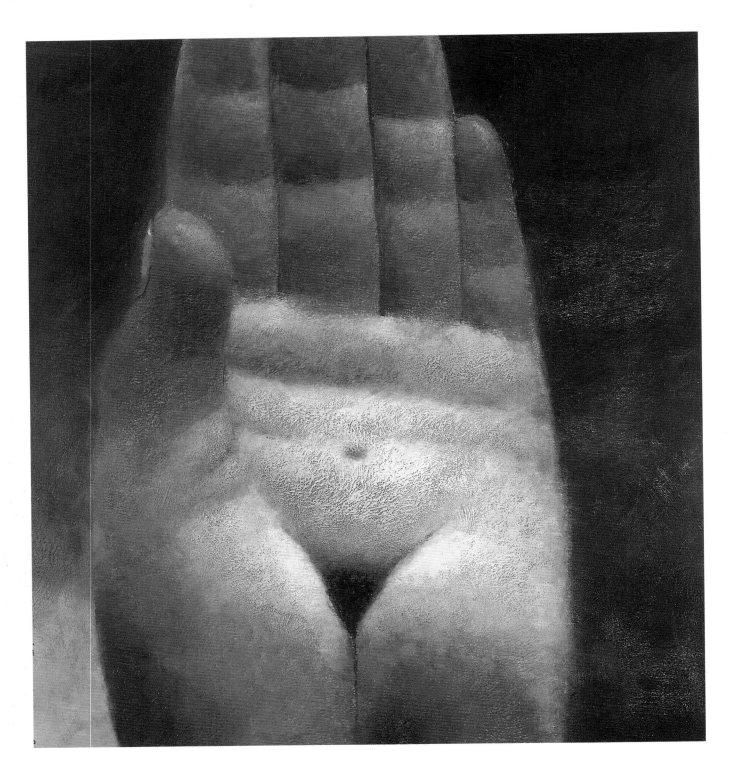

BRAD HOLLAND

JASON HOLLEY

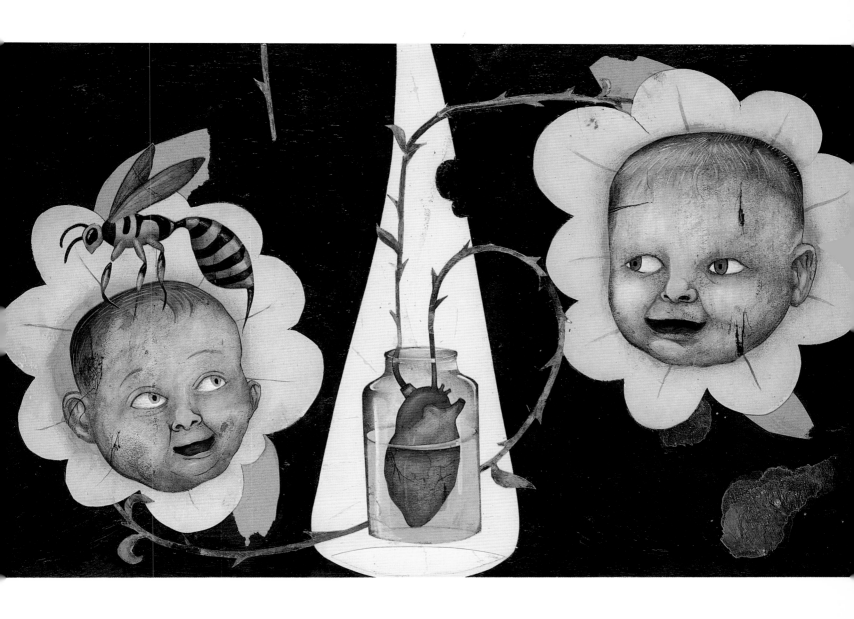

JASON **HOLLEY**

JASON HOLLEY

POST CARD

Correspondence

HADLEY HOOPER

M. KYLE HOLLINGSWORTH

SHE DETERMINED, that IN ANOTHER TIME AND PLACE
HE COULD HAVE BEEN, the SAME PERSON
HERE and N...

DAVID HUGHES

JOHN H. HOWARD

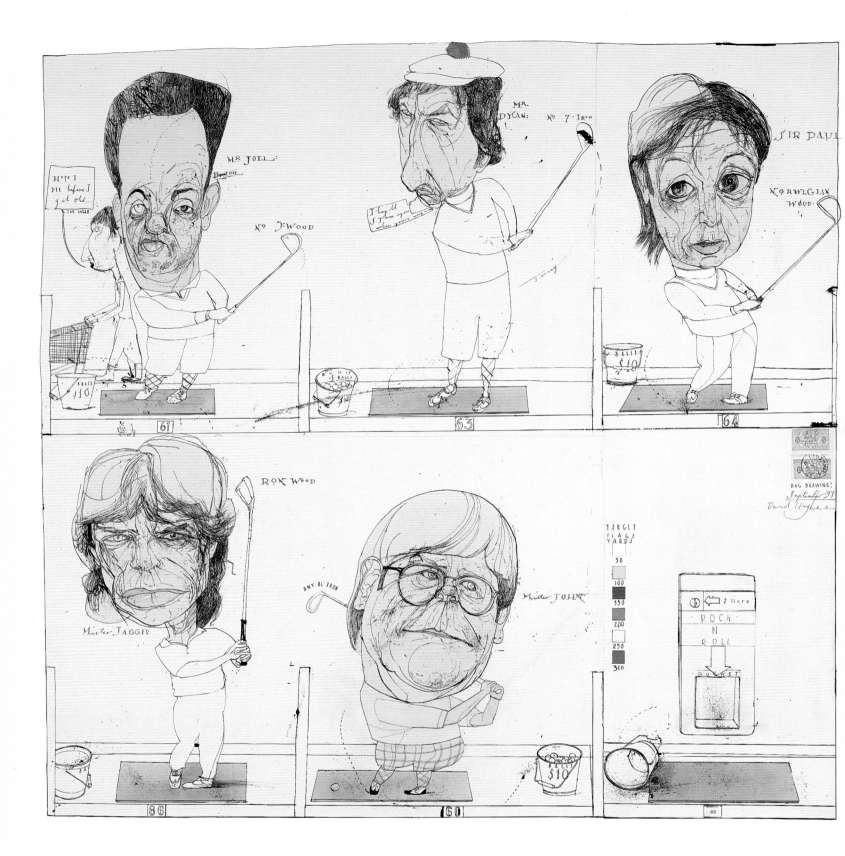

DAVID HUGHES

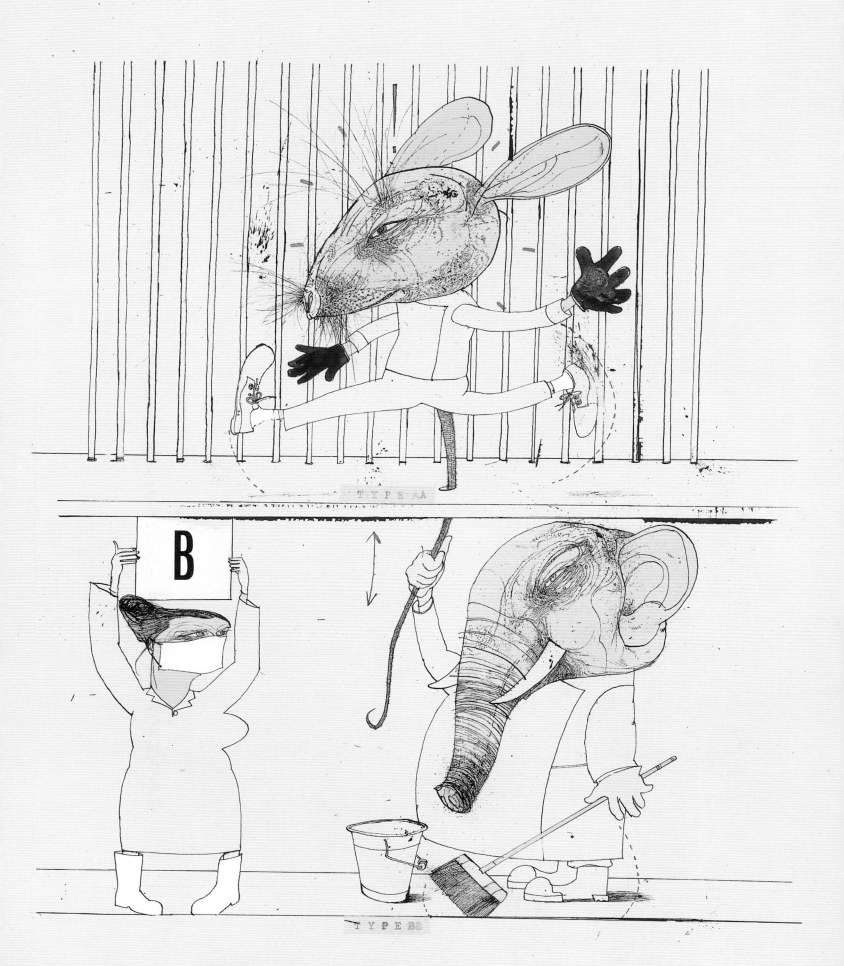

DAVID HUGHES

PHIL HULING

HUNGRY DOG STUDIO

PHIL HULING

HUNGRY DOG STUDIO

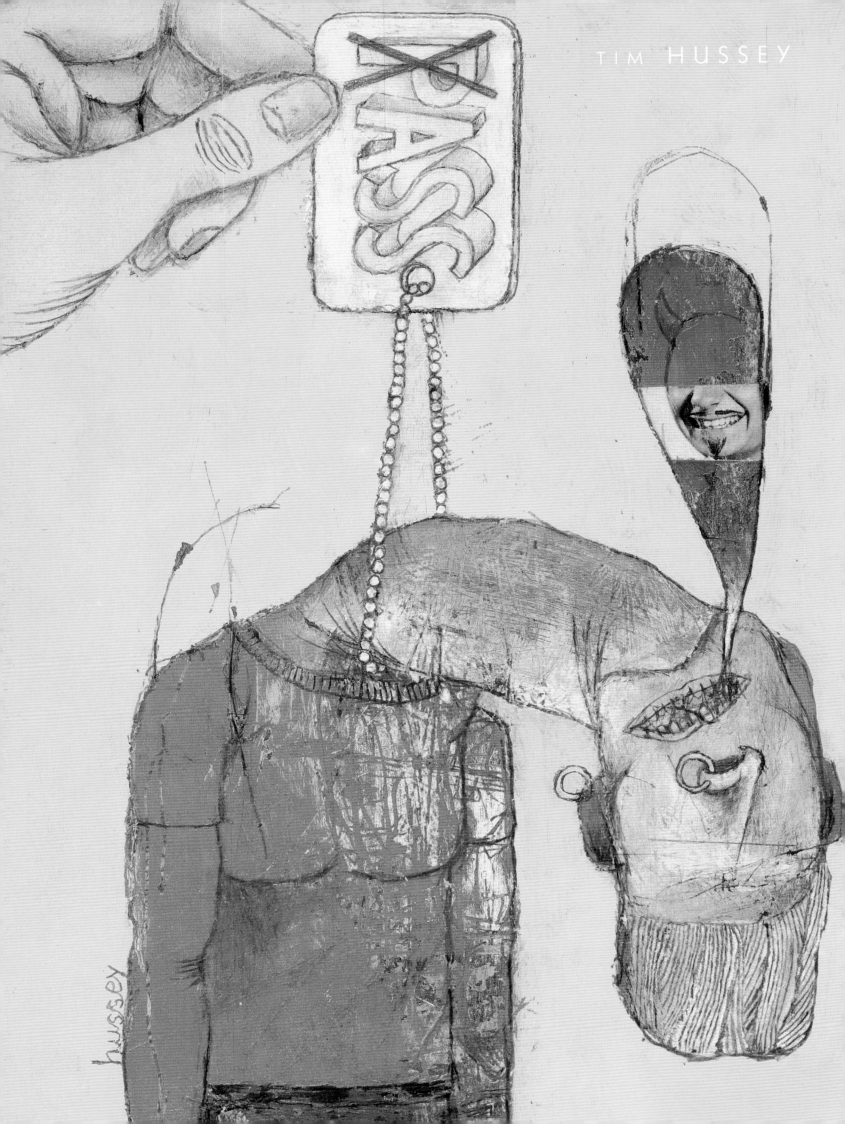

TIM HUSSEY

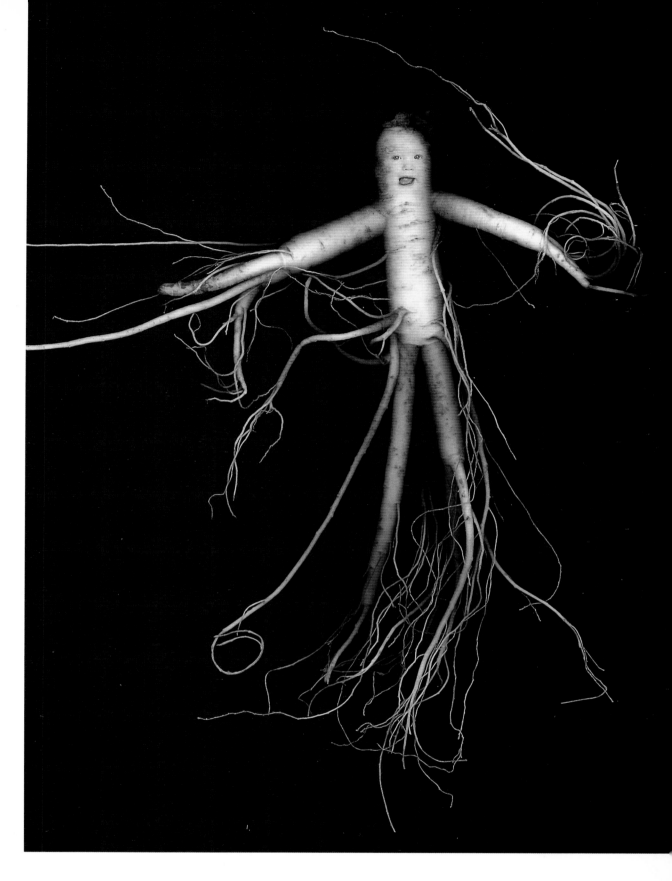

MIRKO ILIĆ

KEI ISHIHARA

JORDIN ISIP

ERIK T. JOHNSON

JOEL PETER **JOHNSON**

TED JOUFLAS

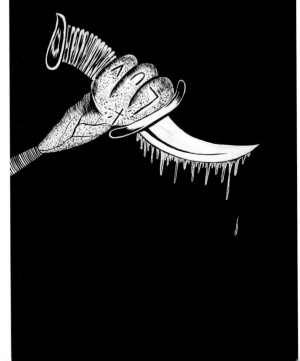

GARY **KELLEY**

WILLIAM **JOYCE**

MICHAEL **KLEIN**

GARY **KELLEY**

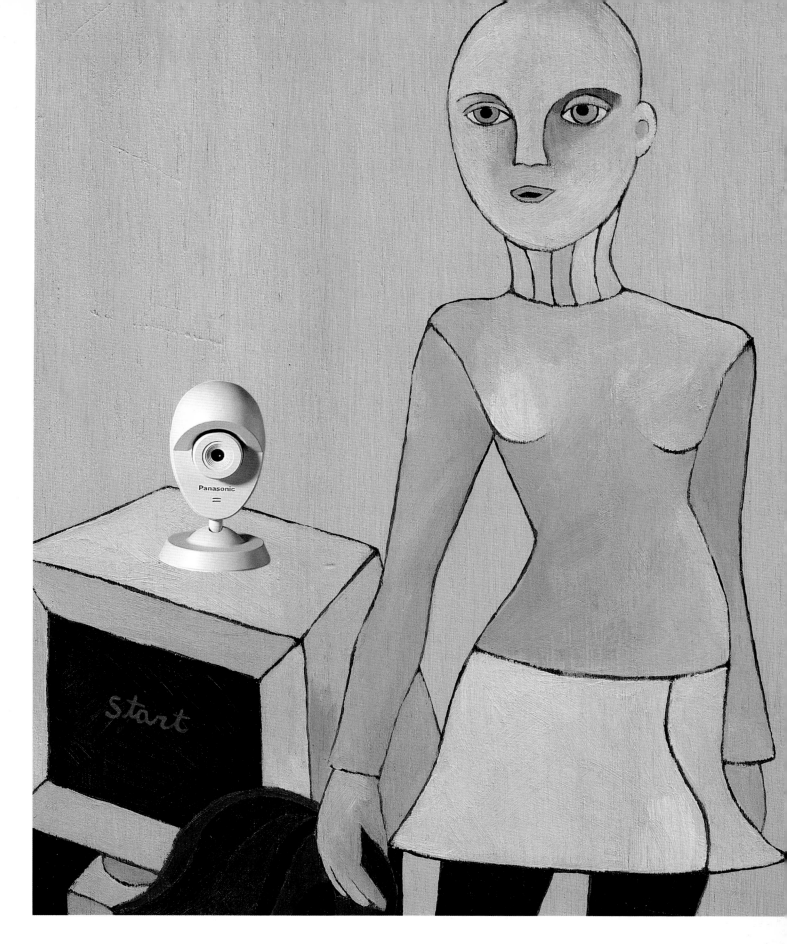

TRISHA **KRAUSS**

ROBERT **KOPECKY**

TRISHA KRAUSS

ANJA KROENCKE

STEPHEN KRONINGER

JULIA KUHL

ANITA KUNZ

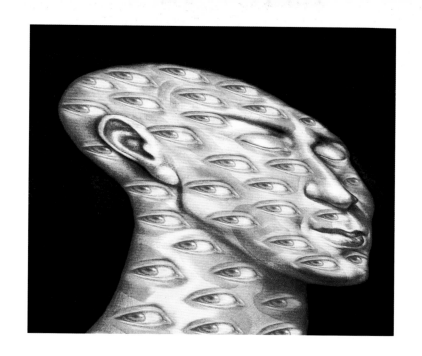

ANITA **KUNZ**

PETER **KUPER**

Lardy.

'a ulmi folia scop

PHILIPPE LARDY

PHILIPPE LARDY

SCOTT LAUMANN

PHILIPPE LARDY

ZOHAR LAZAR

ZOHAR LAZAR

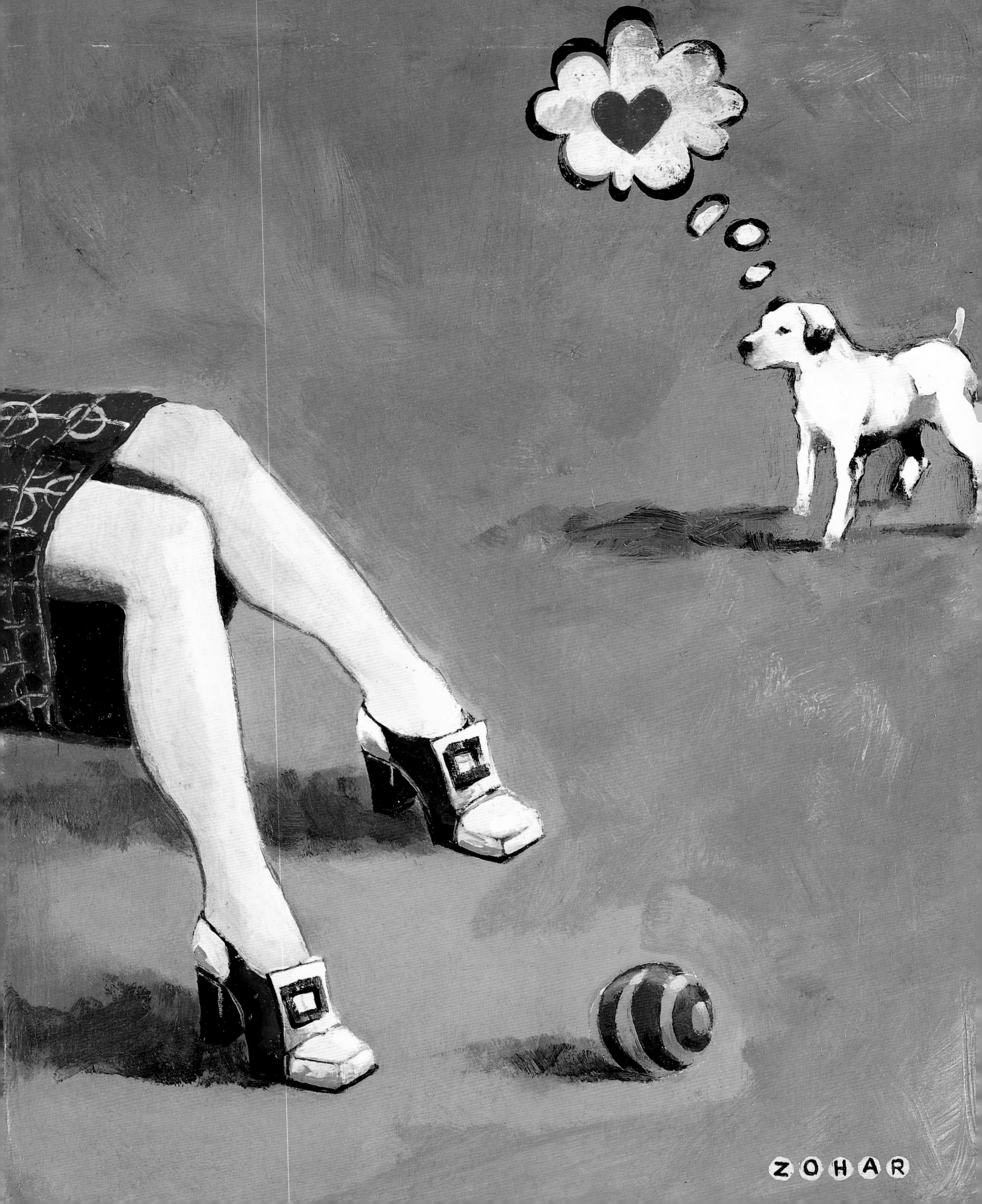

LAURA LEVINE

PIERRE LE-TAN

ROSS MacDONALD

KANDY LITTRELL

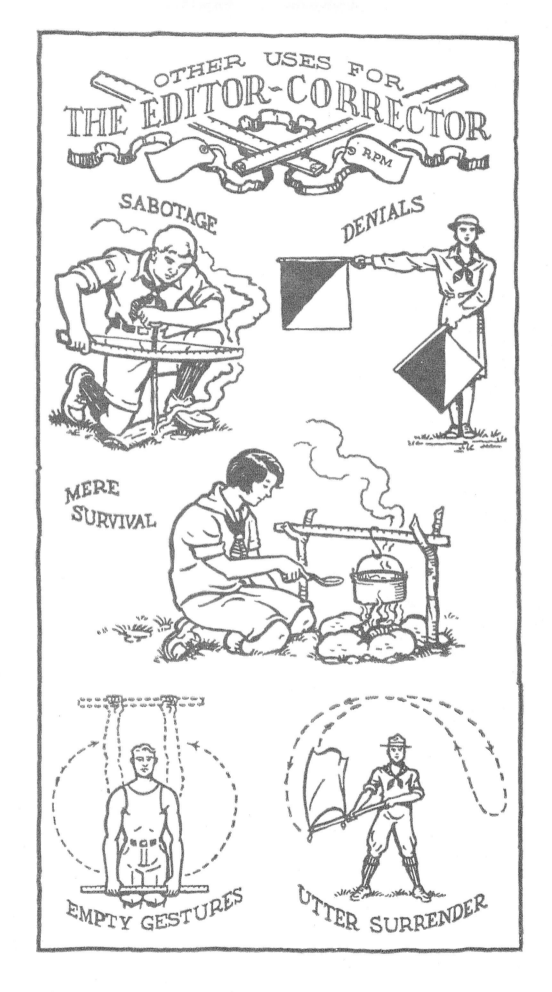

ROSS MacDONALD

ROSS MacDONALD

ROSS MacDONALD

FRANK MADDOCKS

JAMES MARSH

STEPHEN MARQUART

RUTH MARTEN

MATTHEW MARTIN

MATTHEW MARTIN

DAVID MAZZUCCELLI

ADAM McCAULEY

A D A M M c C A U L E Y

CHESLEY
M^cCLAREN

DAVID McLIMANS

JAMES McMULLAN

PRIDE'S CROSSING

BY TINA HOWE
DIRECTED BY JACK O'BRIEN

LINCOLN CENTER THEATER

ah, Wilderness! by Eugene O'Neill

directed by Daniel Sullivan

Lincoln Center Theater

JAMES McMULLAN

AN AMERICAN DAUGHTER

BY WENDY WASSERSTEIN

DIRECTED BY DANIEL SULLIVAN

LINCOLN CENTER THEATER

SCOTT MENCHIN

JOE MORSE

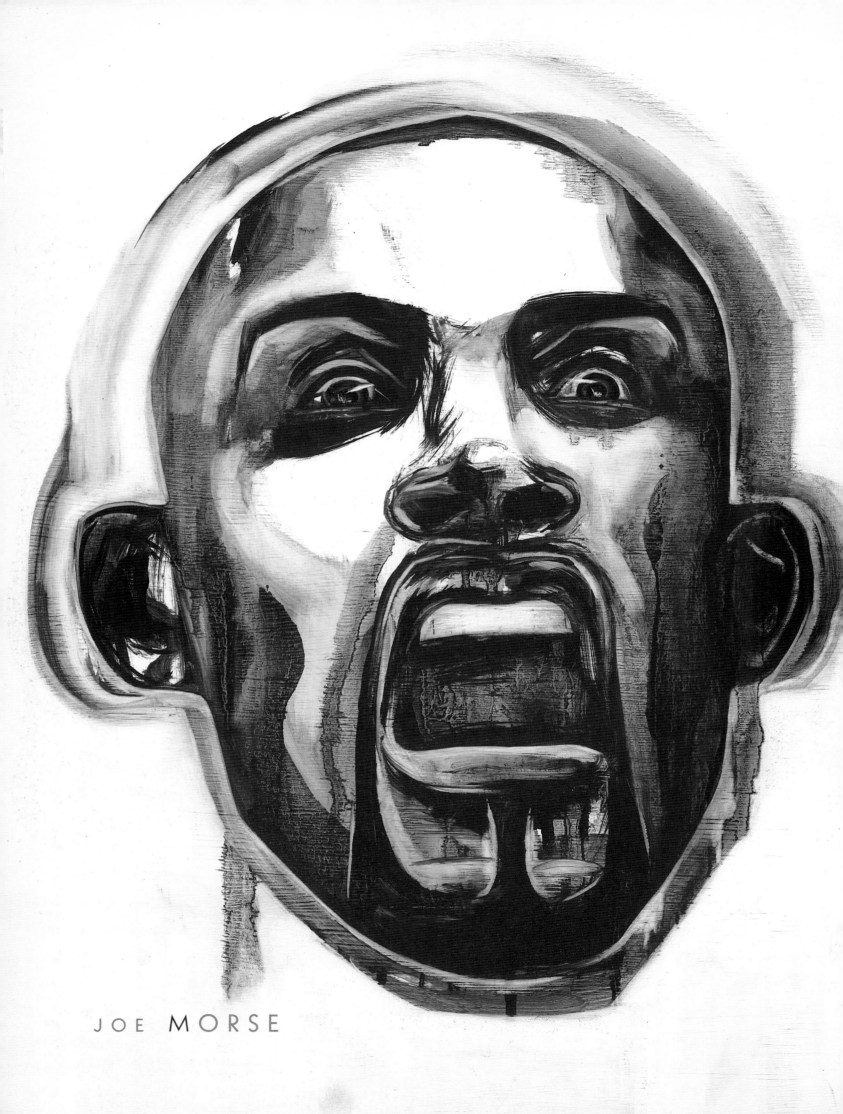

JOE MORSE

JOEL NAKAMURA

CHRISTOPH
NIEMANN

NIXON

CHURCHILL

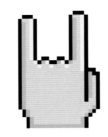

BATMAN

STEVEN SPIELBERG

CHRISTO

GIACOMETTI

PICASSO

MUNCH

PAMELA ANDERSON

KATE MOSS

BRUCE LEE

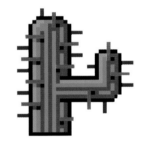

ST. SEBASTIAN

MUHAMMED ALI

ATLAS

CYRANO DE BERGERAC

PELE

CHRISTOPH NIEMANN

CHRISTIAN NORTHEAST

CHRISTIAN NORTHEAST

CHRISTIAN NORTHEAST

CHRISTIAN NORTHEAST

TIM O'BRIEN

FILIP PAGOWSKI

F

GARY PANTER

C. F. PAYNE

ROBERTO PARADA

C. F. PAYNE

ALAIN PILON

ALAIN PILON

DAVID PLUNKERT

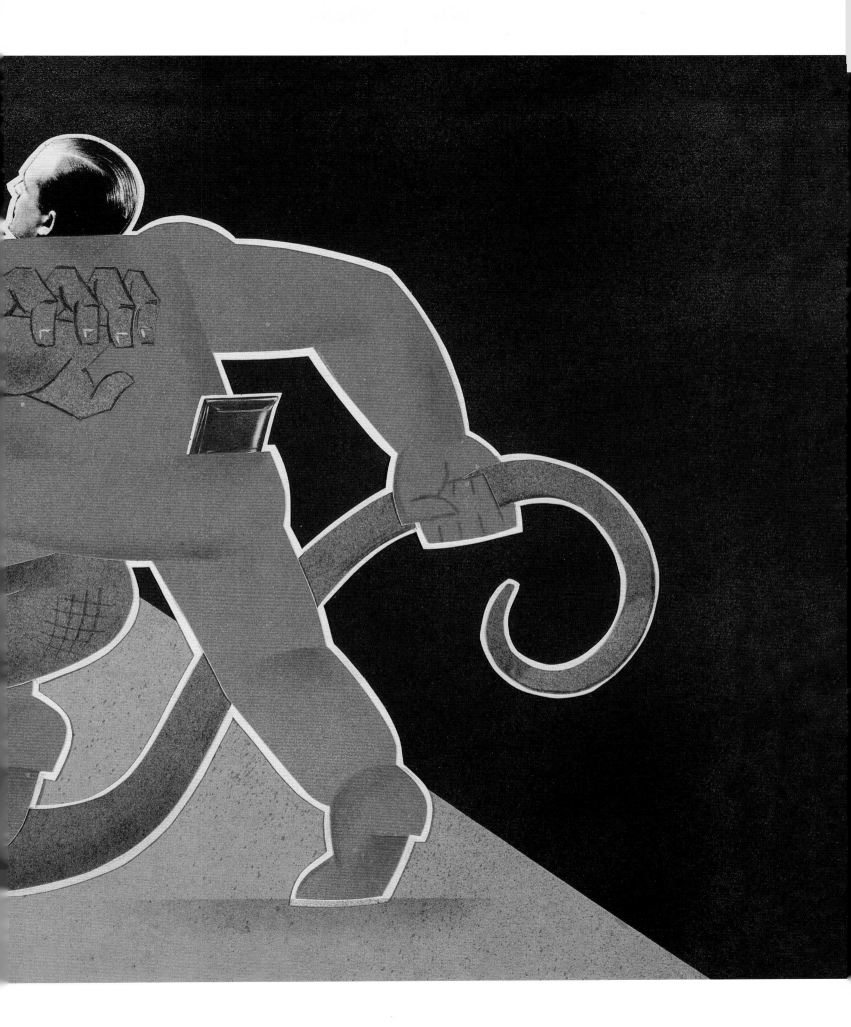

DAVID PLUNKERT

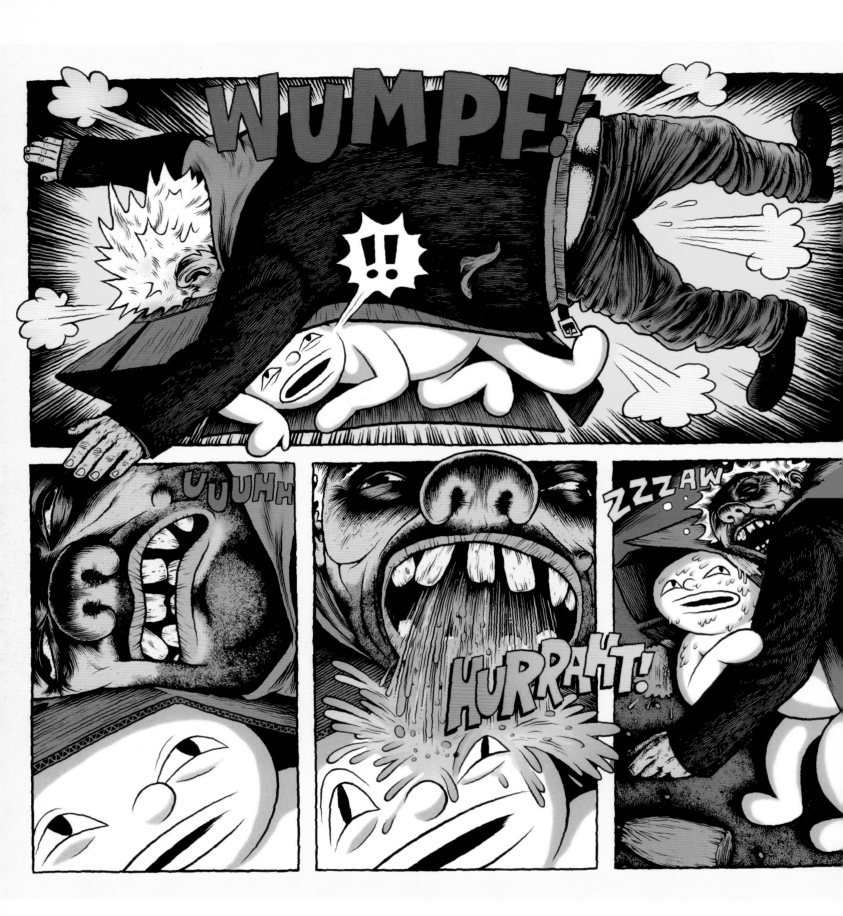

ARCHER PREWITT

DEMETRIOS PSILLOS

LIZ PYLE

CHRIS PYLE

JOHN RITTER

ANDY RASH

VICTORIA **ROBERTS**

IRENE ROFHEART-PIGOTT

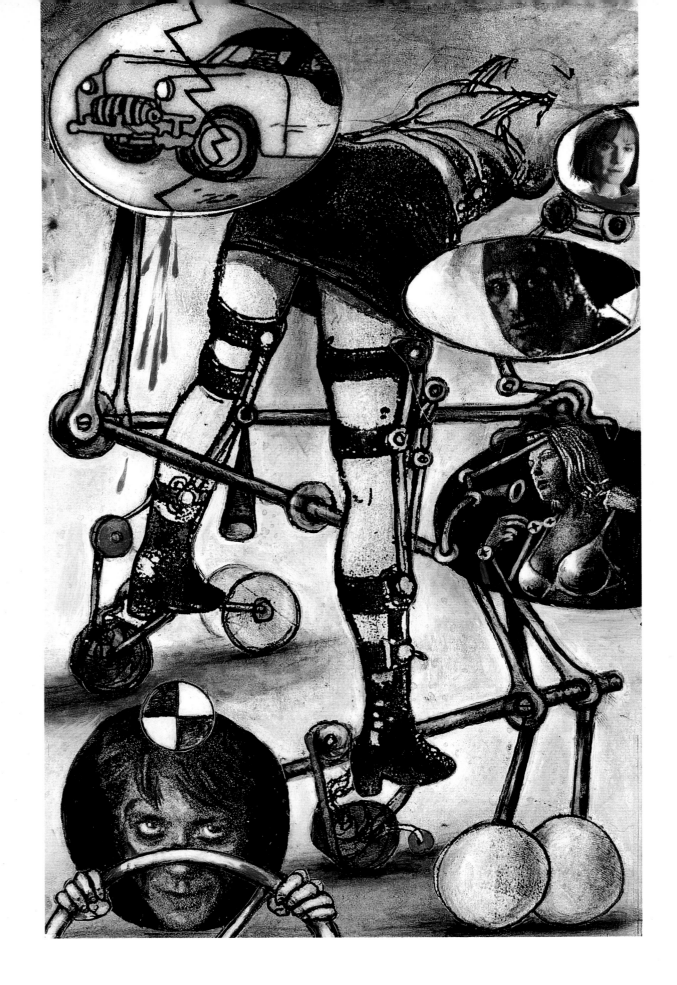

JONATHON ROSEN

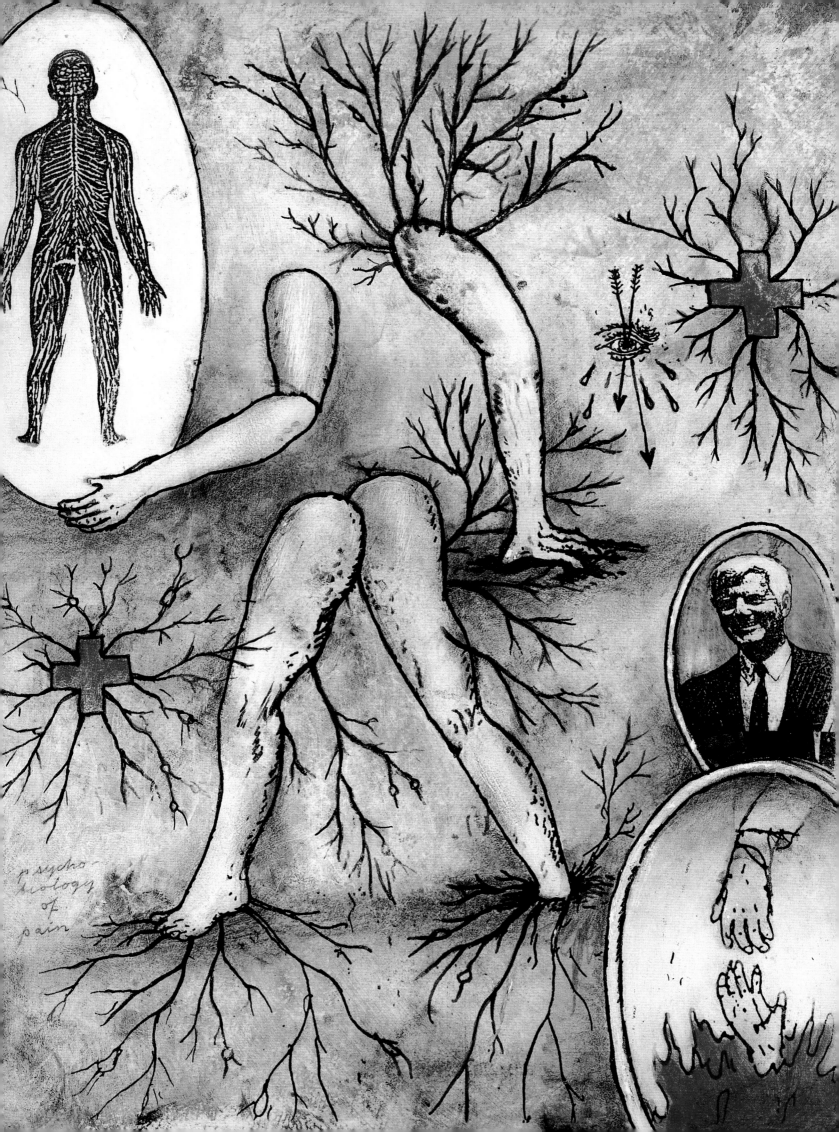

psycho
biology
of
pain

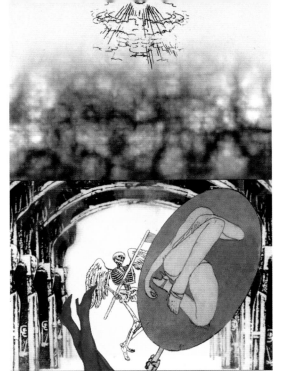

JONATHON ROSEN

MARK RYDEN

JOSEPH SALINA

STEPHEN SAVAGE

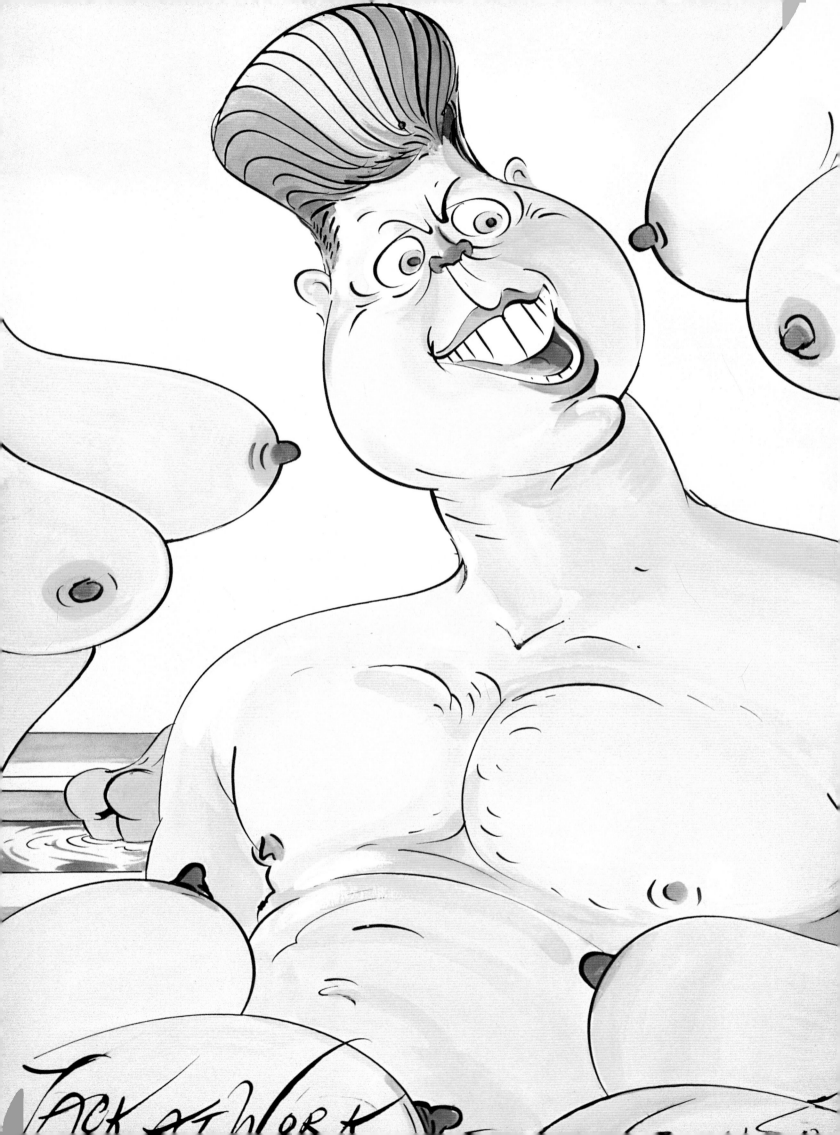

JACK AT WORK

WARD SCHUMAKER

GERALD SCARFE

SARA L. SCHWARTZ

MICHAEL SCHWAB

J J SEDELMAIER

J. OTTO SEIBOLD

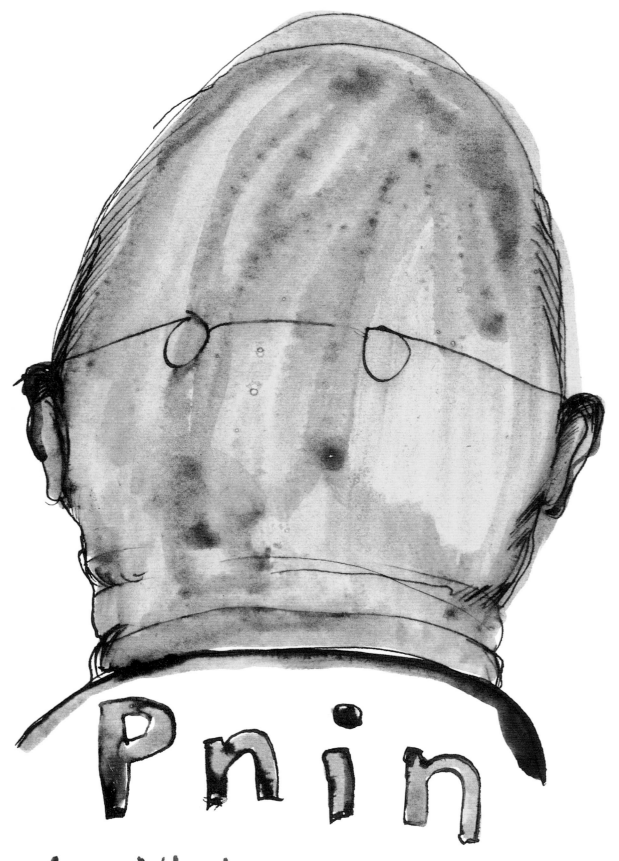

Pnin

by Vladimir Nabokov.

LEANNE SHAPTON

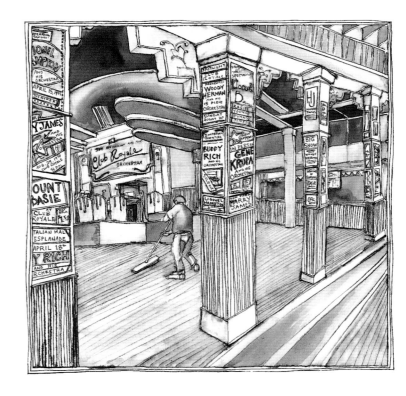

LEANNE SHAPTON

CHRIS SHARP

DAVID K. SHELDON

WHITNEY SHERMAN

A SKWISH

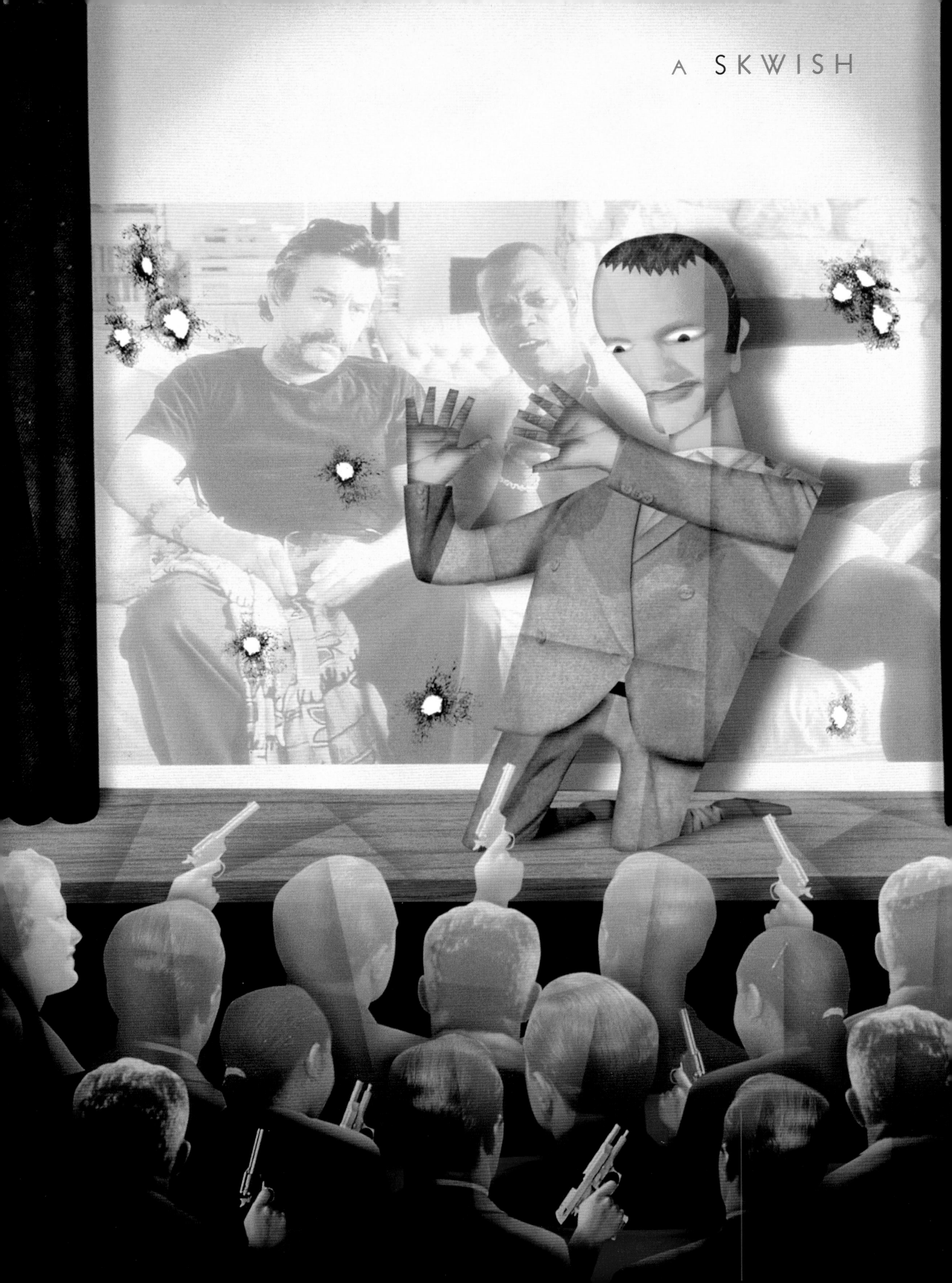

OWEN SMITH

FICTION ISSUE

O Smith

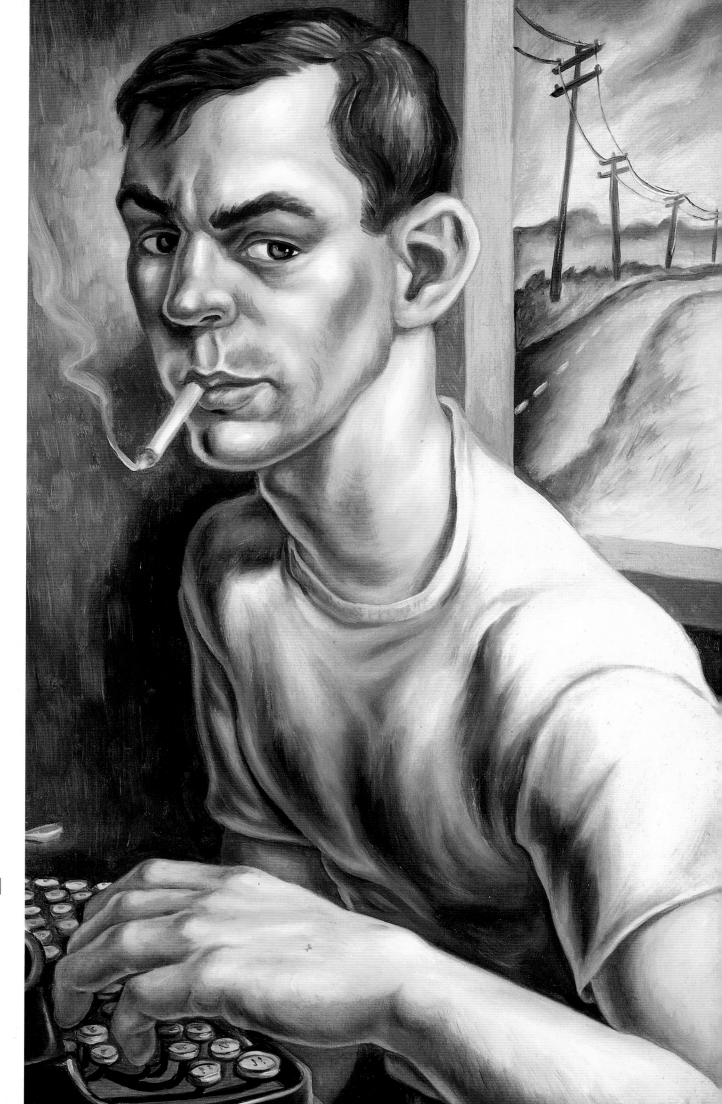

OWEN
SMITH

E D W A R D
SOREL

JOE SORREN

MARCOS SORENSEN

JOE SORREN

GREG SPALENKA

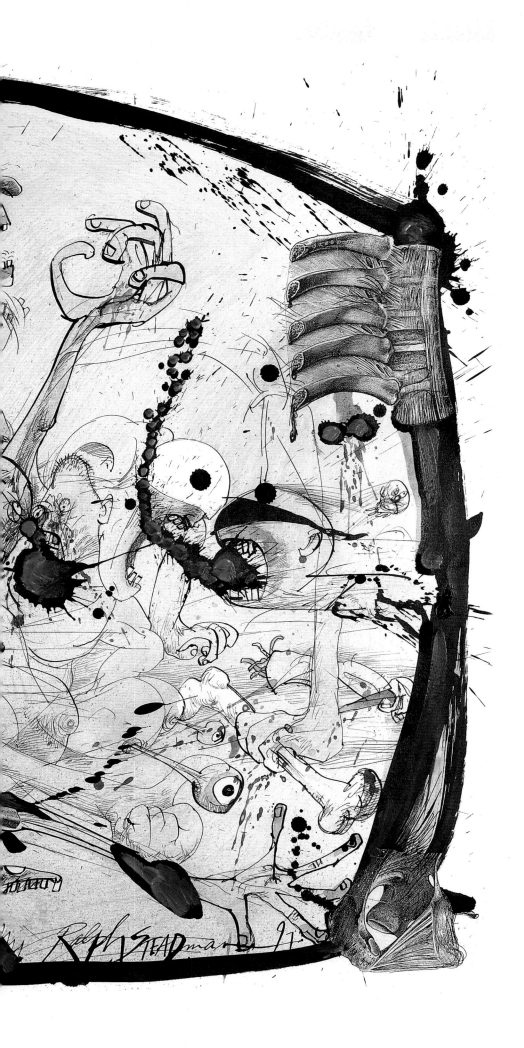

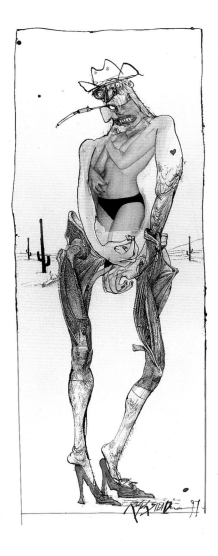

RALPH
STEADMAN

JAMES STEINBERG

CHIMPANZEE
STERMER

DUGALD STERMER

DONALD SULTAN

WARD SUTTON

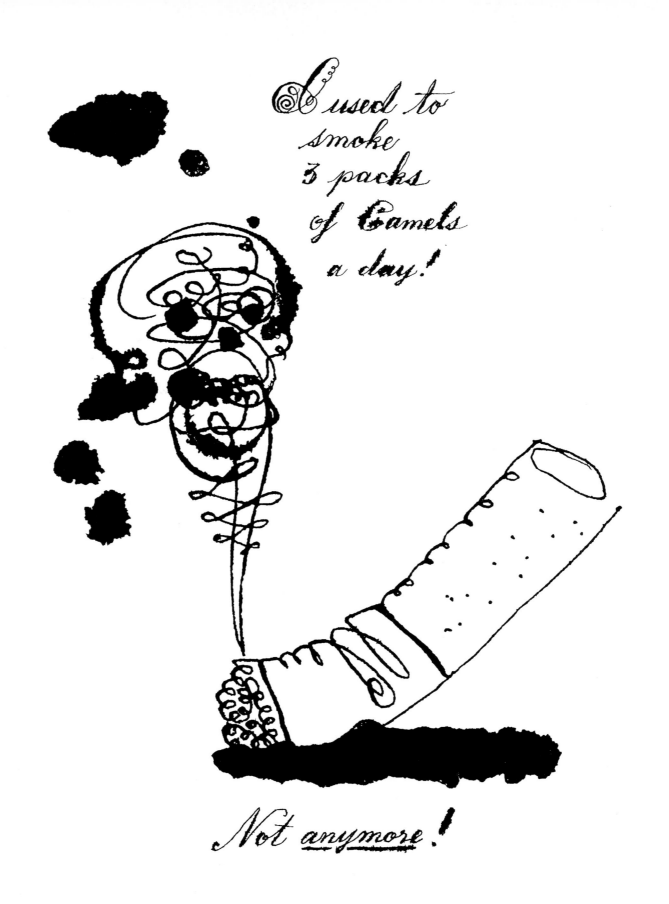

I used to
smoke
3 packs
of Camels
a day!

Not anymore!

ELVIS SWIFT

HIROSHI TANABE

HIROSHI TANABE

AMY TANNER

GARY TAXALI

MARK TODD & ESTHER WATSON

MARK TODD

GREG TUCKER

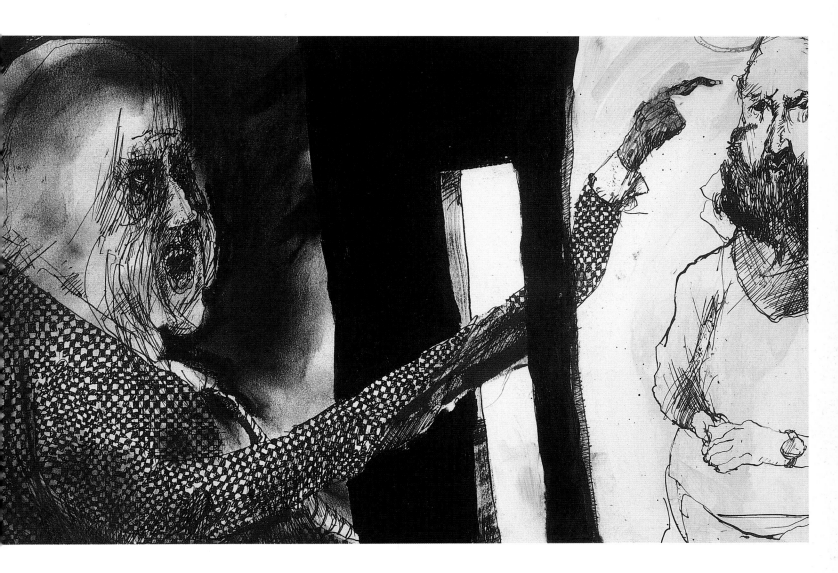

JONATHAN **TWINGLEY**

MARK ULRIKSEN

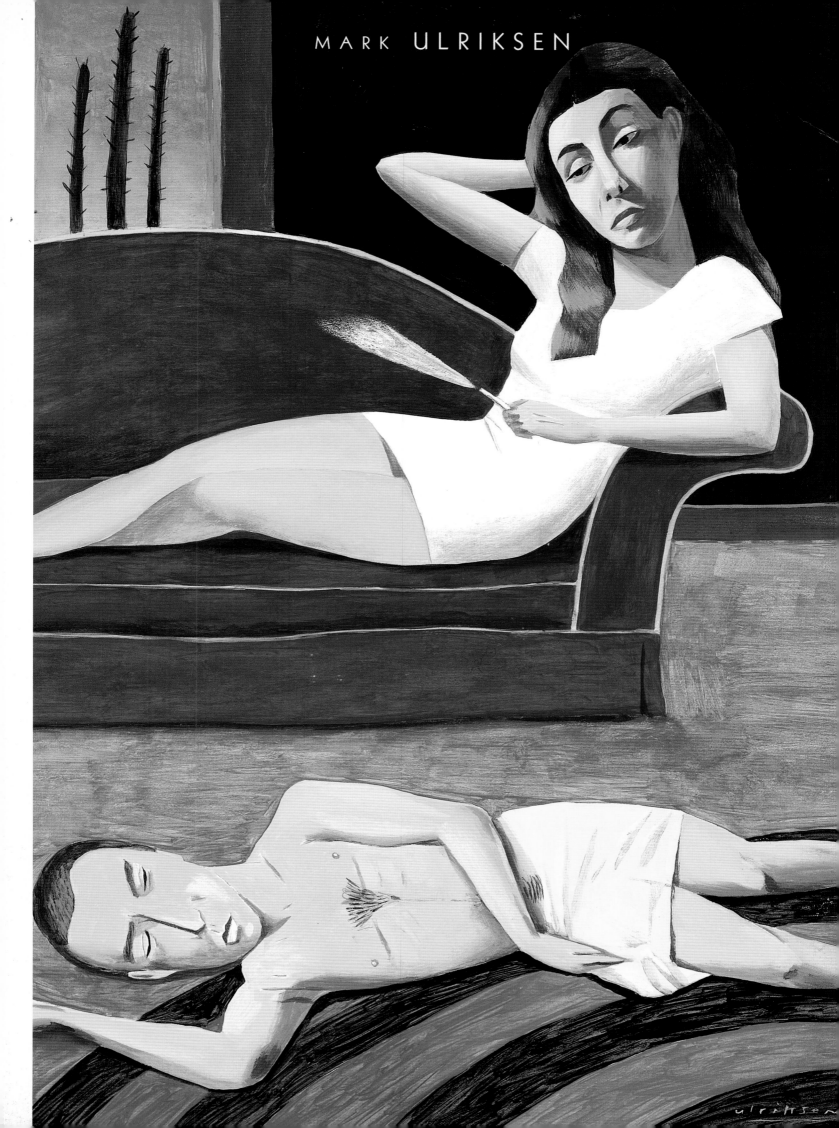

MARK ULRIKSEN

MARK ULRIKSEN

JACK UNRUH

girlfriend

CHRIS VAN DUSEN

RICCARDO
VECCHIO

RICCARDO VECCHIO

MAURICE VELLEKOOP

ANDREA VENTURA

JAMES VICTORE

STEFANO VITALE

CYNTHIA VON BUHLER

CHRIS WARE

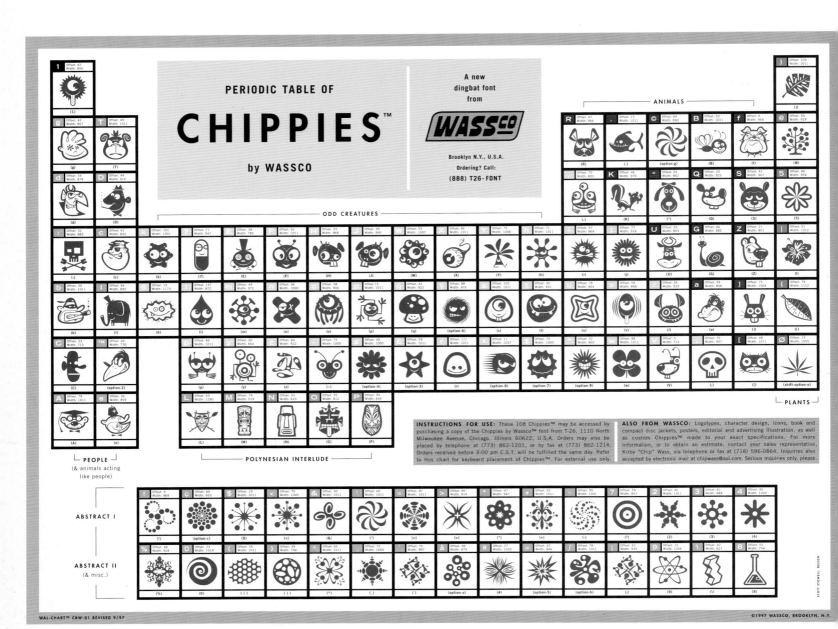

CHIP WASS

ESTHER WATSON

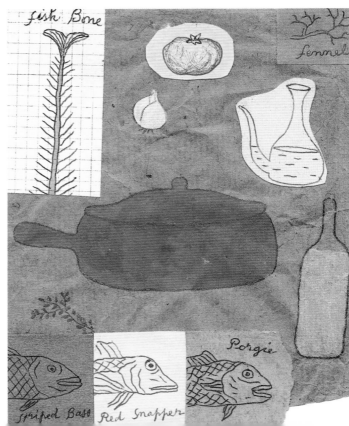

PHILIPPE WEISBECKER

LEIGH **WELLS**

MICHAEL S. **WERTZ**

ERIC WHITE

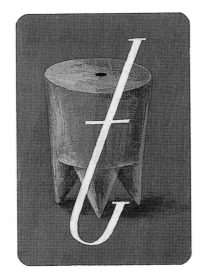

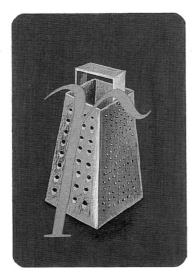

NOAH WOODS

DAN YACCARINO

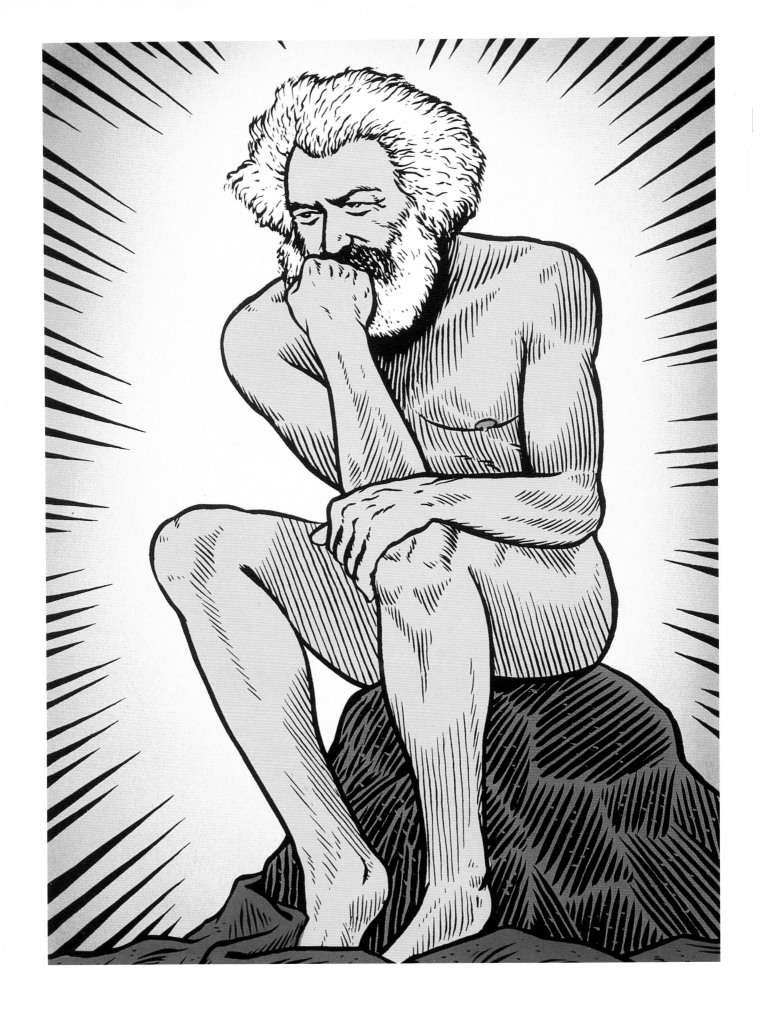

MARK ZINGARELLI   BOB ZOELL

MICK AARESTRUP

8784 1/2 Rangely Avenue
Los Angeles, CA 90048

8

Illustration for the article "Personal Test", September 1997.

Publication:
MEN'S FITNESS

Art Director:
DEAN ABATEMARCO

Designer:
FRANKIE HOLT

Publishing Company:
Weider Publications

DANIEL ADEL

56 West 22nd Street 8th Floor
New York, NY 10010
212-989-6114

9

Bill Gates, Michael Eisner and Robert Murdoch for the 'Power 101 Issue', October 31, 1997, entitled 'Witche$ Brew'.

Publication:
ENTERTAINMENT WEEKLY

Design Director:
JOHN KORPICS

Art Director:
GERALDINE HESSLER

Publishing Company:
Time Inc.

DOUG AITKEN

49 Ann Street 3rd Floor
New York, NY 10038
NY 212-608-1965
LA 310-378-7055

10, 11

One from a series illustrating each letter of the alphabet.

Client:
EMPORIO ARMANI

Designer:
DAVID CARSON

Design Firm:
David Carson Design

JULIAN ALLEN

1714 Bolton Street
Baltimore, MD 21217

12-13

Dodger's legend Jackie Robinson as he joins the major league, for the article "The Breakthrough", May 5th 1997.

Publication:
SPORTS ILLUSTRATED

Creative Director:
STEVEN HOFFMAN

Editor:
BILL COLSON

Publishing Company:
Time Inc.

TERRY ALLEN

84 Campfire Road
Chappaqua, NY 10514
914-238-1422

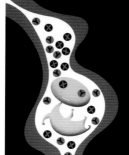

14

Illustration for the article "Wo/Man", May/June 1997.

Publication:
STANFORD MEDICAL MAGAZINE

Art Director:
PAUL CARSTENSEN

Designer:
ANDREW DANISH

Editor:
BOB COHN

Publishing Company:
Stanford University

CHARLES S. ANDERSON

30 North 1st Street
Minneapolis, MN 55401

15

Poster to announce a lecture given by the designer.

Client:
ART DIRECTORS CLUB OF PHILADELPHIA

Art Director:
CHARLES S. ANDERSON

Designer:
CHARLES S. ANDERSON

Design Firm:
Charles S. Anderson Design Co.

16

Illustration for the feature "Jammed Together Names, Inc.", July 20, 1997.

Publication:
THE NEW YORK TIMES MAGAZINE

Art Director:
JANET FROELICH

Publishing Company:
The New York Times Co.

17

Illustration announcing the American Museum of Natural History's exhibit 'Endangered!'

Publication:
NEW YORK MAGAZINE

Design Director:
ROBERT NEWMAN

Art Directors:
FLORIAN BACHLEDA AND PINO IMPASTATO

Publishing Company:
Primedia Inc.

CHARLES S. ANDERSON

30 North 1st Street
Minneapolis, MN 55401

18

Illustration for a children's computer greeting card, called 'D-Cards On-line'.

Client:
THE WALT DISNEY CO.

Art Director:
LISA MICHURSKI*

CARLOS APONTE

130 West 25th Street
New York, NY 10010
212-414-1697

19

TV spot of a chicken and his band being pelted with eggs when they get caught lip-synching.

Client:
BANCO POPULAR

Art Directors:
R.O. BLECHMAN AND NORMA JEAN COLBERG

Designer:
CARLOS APONTE

Animator:
TISSA DAVID

Agency:
BADILLO NAZCA SAATCHI & SAATCHI

Producers:
MARGARITA SOROETA AND BRIAN O'CONNELL

Production Company:
The Ink Tank

PATRICK ARRASMITH

309 Sixth Street #3
Brooklyn, NY 11215
718-499-4101

20-21

Illustration for the article "Collective Guilt", September 1, 1997, a story about the medical community's performance in South Africa during the apartheid.

Publication:
AMERICAN MEDICAL NEWS

Art Director:
JEF CAPALDI

Designer:
JEF CAPALDI

Publishing Company:
American Medical News

N. ASCENCIOS

918 Metropolitan Avenue #1-L
Brooklyn, NY 11211
718-388-7931

22

'Cinderella', January 1998.

Publication:
PRO ILLUSTRATION II

Art Director:
JILL BOSSERT

Publishing Company:
Society of Illustrators

23

Portrait of Oprah Winfrey for "The Crusader", March 21, 1997, an article on how she resurrected America's interest in reading with her on-air book club.

Publication:
ENTERTAINMENT WEEKLY

Design Director:
JOHN KORPICS

Designer:
DIRK BARRNETT

Publishing Company:
Time Inc.

ISTVAN BANYAI

666 Greenwich Street #420
New York, NY 10014
212-627-2953

24

Illustration for "'O' Yes", November 1997, where twelve women described their best lovers.

Publication:
DETAILS

Design Director:
ROBERT NEWMAN

Designer:
MARLENE SEZNI

Publishing Company:
Condé Nast Publications, Inc.

Illustration for the article "Sex, Home & Videotapes", where it w discovered that the best way to participate in the sex-video revolution is to do it yourself.

Publication:
PLAYBOY

Art Directors:
TOM STAEBLER AND KERIG POPE

Publishing Company:
Playboy Enterprises, Inc.

KAREN BARBOUR

P.O. Box 1210
Point Reyes Station, CA 94956
415-663-1100

Personal piece.

Personal piece.

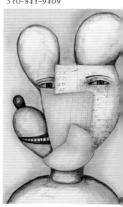

Personal piece.

DEBORAH BARRET

111-A Tamalpais Road
Berkeley, CA 94708
510-841-9409

Self-promotional piece.

-promotional piece.

29

30

...coleta String Quartet', a ...sonal piece inspired by ...isit to Recoleta Cemetery in ...nos Aires.

...CHAEL BARTALOS
... Ramona Avenue #2
... Francisco, CA 94103-2292
...5-863-4569

31

...ver image entitled 'You Don't ...ow Jack', Fall 1997.
...blication:
BLAB! #9
... Director:
...ONTE BEAUCHAMP
...signer:
...ONTE BEAUCHAMP
...itor:
...ONTE BEAUCHAMP
...blishing Company:
...ntagraphics

...ARY BASEMAN
...4 North Formosa Avenue
... Angeles, CA 90036
...3-934-5567

32-33

Illustration entitled 'What's Your Pleasure', for the MTV Video Awards Program Book.
Publication:
FETISH &
Client:
MERCURY RECORDS-MTV VIDEO MUSIC AWARDS
Art Director:
JEFF SCHULZ

LOU BEACH
900 South Tremaine Avenue
Los Angeles, CA 90019
213-934-7335 Tel.
213-934-1030 Fax.

Endpapers.

MELINDA BECK
536 5th Street #2
Brooklyn, NY 11215
718-499-0985

34

Illustration for "Missionary Work at the Export-Import Bank", an article about hand-outs at the World Bank.
Publication:
THE PROGRESSIVE
Art Director:
PATRICK J.B. FLYNN
Designer:
PATRICK J.B. FLYNN
Editor:
MATTHEW ROTHSCHILD

35

Calendar, illustrating the quote "Silence is like starvation. Don't be fooled. It's nothing short of that, and felt most strongly when one has had a full belly most of her life." –Cherrie Moraga.
Client:
THE PROGRESSIVE
Art Director:
PATRICK J.B. FLYNN
Designer:
PATRICK J.B. FLYNN

POLLY BECKER
156 West Newton Street
Boston, MA 02118
617-247-0469

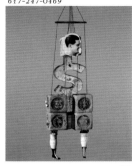

36

Illustration interpreting the song 'Dolls Dollars' by the band Suran Song in Stag, for the benefit CD 'Nigh'.
Art Director:
CYNTHIA VON BUHLER
Design Firm:
Stoltze Design

WESLEY BEDROSIAN
302 Metropolitan Avenue #2
Brooklyn, NY 11211
718-782-5018

37

Personal piece.

BENOÎT
c/o Riley Illustration
155 West 15th Street
New York, NY 10011
212-989-8770

38

Illustration for "The Millennium Notebook" feature, June 30, 1997. Copyline: "Checking to see when the cows come home."
Publication:
NEWSWEEK
Art Director:
AMID CAPECI
Publishing Company:
Newsweek, Inc.

39

Illustration for "The Millennium Notebook" feature, January 10, 1998. Copyline: "Bring me the next mystery to solve."
Publication:
NEWSWEEK
Art Director:
AMID CAPECI
Publishing Company:
Newsweek, Inc.

GUY BILLOUT
225 Lafayette Street, Room 1008
New York, NY 10012
212-431-6350

40-41

Part of a series for "The Great Climate Flip-Flop", January 1998, a story about changes in the climate.
Publication:
THE ATLANTIC MONTHLY
Art Director:
JUDY GARLAN
Publishing Company:
The Atlantic Monthly

R.O. BLECHMAN
2 West 47th Street
New York, NY 10036
212-869-1630

42-43

Selections from the two books 'The Life of Saint Nicholas' and 'The Book of Jonah'.
Art Director:
R.O. BLECHMAN
Designer:
R.O. BLECHMAN
Editor:
LINDA SUNSHINE
Author:
R.O. BLECHMAN
Publishing Company:
Stewart, Tabori & Chang

BARRY BLITT
34 Lincoln Avenue
Greenwich, CT. 06830

44

Cover art. A visual pun entitled "Doorman", November 17, 1997.
Publication:
THE NEW YORKER
Art Editor:
FRANÇOISE MOULY
Publishing Company:
Condé Nast Publications, Inc.

45

Businessperson's portrait constructed from the sum of his tasks, for the article "Project You", December/January 1998.
Publication:
FAST COMPANY MAGAZINE
Art Director:
PATRICK MITCHELL
Designer:
PATRICK MITCHELL
Editor:
ALAN M. WEBBER

45

Illustration for the article "Are You a Performance Pig?", May/June 1997, one in a series which used animals to describe different investor "types".
Publication:
BLOOMBERG PERSONAL FINANCE
Art Director:
CAROL LAYTON
Designers:
CAROL LAYTON AND SANDY O'CONNOR
Editor:
WILLIAM H. INMAN
Captions:
BARRY BLITT

JULIETTE BORDA
114 Carnegie Place
Pittsburgh, PA 15208
412-441-7188

46

Illustration for "Beauty RX – Flake Off", March 2, 1998, a beauty advice story.
Publication:
JUMP MAGAZINE
Art Director:
CHRYSTAL FALCIONI
Designer:
JENNIFER SIDEL
Editor:
LORI BERGER
Publishing Company:
Weider Publications, Inc.

47

Illustration for "Arc of the Diver", July 1997, an article about a female cliff diving champion.
Publication:
SHAPE MAGAZINE
Art Director:
DONNA GIOVANNITTI
Editor:
BARBARA HARRIS
Publishing Company:
Weider Publications, Inc.

48

Illustration for "Under Your Thumb", October 1997, an article about wife-guarding.
Publication:
ESQUIRE
Design Director:
ROBERT PRIEST
Art Director:
ROCKWELL HARWOOD
Editor:
DAVID GRANGER
Publishing Company:
The Hearst Corporation

49

Illustration for a fiction piece entitled "The Lunatic, the Lover and the Poet", March 1998.

Publication:
THE ATLANTIC
MONTHLY

Art Director:
JUDY GARLAN

Publishing Company:
The Atlantic Monthly

TIM BOWER

61 Pearl Street #306
Brooklyn, NY 11201
718-834-8974

50

Portrait of Allen Ginsburg for "Remembering Allen", May 29, 1997, a tribute to the American poet upon his death on April 5th.

Publication:
ROLLING STONE

Art Director:
FRED WOODWARD

Publishing Company:
Wenner Media, Inc.

51

Portrait of the late Tupac Shakur for "Thug Life After Death", January 22, 1998, a review of his posthumously released album 'R U Still Down?'.

Publication:
ROLLING STONE

Art Director:
FRED WOODWARD

Deputy Art Director:
GAIL ANDERSON

Publishing Company:
Wenner Media, Inc.

52

Opening illustration for the fiction piece "The Prisoner", Summer 1997.

Publication:
SMOKE MAGAZINE

Art Director:
ALYSON BOXMAN

Editor:
ALYSON BOXMAN

Publishing Company:
Lockwood Publishing

52

Illustration for "To Catch a Killer", a report on Mir Aimal Kansi who was brought back from Pakistan to stand trial on the killing of two CIA employees.

Publication:
GQ

Art Director:
JOHN BOYER

Publishing Company:
Condé Nast Publications, Inc.

DAVID M. BRINLEY

122 West Mill Station Drive
Newark, DE 19711
302-731-9485

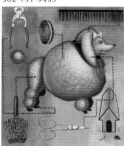

53

Illustration for a prison poodle grooming contest poster.

Art Director:
JASON HOLLEY

STEVE BRODNER

120 Cabrini Boulevard #116
New York, NY 10033
212-740-8174

52

Cover illustration for the feature "The Madness of Speaker Newt", March 17, 1997.

Publication:
THE NEW REPUBLIC

Art Director:
ERIC BAKER

Designer:
ERIC BAKER

Editor:
MICHAEL KELLY

Publishing Company:
Will Lippincott Publisher

54

Portrait of Tupac Shakur for a review of his posthumously released movie 'Gridlock'd', February 6, 1997.

Publication:
ROLLING STONE

Art Director:
FRED WOODWARD

Deputy Art Director:
GAIL ANDERSON

Publishing Company:
Wenner Media, Inc.

55

Portrait of gossip biographer Kitty Kelley for the feature "Kitty Zipper".

Publication:
THE NEW YORKER

Illustration Director:
CHRIS CURRY

Publishing Company:
Condé Nast Publications, Inc.

56-57

One from a series for "A Pit Bull, a Border Collie and a Show Horse", a campaign sketchbook covering the New York City 1997 Mayoral election.

Publication:
NEW YORK MAGAZINE

Design Director:
MARK MICHAELSON

Art Director:
FLORIAN BACHLEDA

Publishing Company:
Primedia, Inc.

CALEF BROWN

12761 Caswell Avenue
Los Angeles, CA 90066
310-397-7603

58

Commissioned, yet unused character created for a line of jeans called "Daddy", April 1997.

Client:
UNION BAY

Art Director:
JASON SKINNER

Design Firm:
Toth Design

59

Illustration for a paper promotion interpreting the Chinese astrological sign of the horse.

Client:
SPICERS PAPER

Art Director:
SCOTT LAMBERT

Designer:
SCOTT LAMBERT

Design Firm:
Martin Design Associates

60

Illustration for the article "Living the Cyborg Life", April 18, 1997.

Publication:
L.A. WEEKLY

Art Director:
BILL SMITH

Designer:
JEFF MONZEL

Editor:
SUE HORTON

Publishing Company:
Stern Publishing, Inc.

60

Painting interpreting the song 'Hopp on Popp' by the band Veronica Black Worpheous Nipple, for the benefit CD 'Nigh'.

Art Director:
CYNTHIA VON BUHLER

Design Firm:
Stoltze Design

ALLAN M. BURCH

404 Red Maple
Kirbyville, MO 65679
417-335-2410

61

Self-portrait entitled 'Arrangement in Green'.

Client:
THEISPOT

PHILIP BURKE

1948 Juron Drive
Niagara Falls, NY 14304

Portrait of President Bill Clinton

Publication:
THE NEW YORKER

Illustration Director:
CHRIS CURRY

Publishing Company:
Condé Nast Publications, I...

Portrait of director Roman Polanski for the article "Polans... Obsession", July 1997, a reply... the editors from Samantha Gein... the woman Polanski was accus... of raping in 1977.

Publication:
VANITY FAIR

Art Director:
DAVID HARRIS

Designer:
JOHN DIXON

Publishing Company:
Condé Nast Publications, I...

FRANCISCO CACERES

1790 Fell Street
San Francisco, CA 94117
415-776-6413

Illustration for "An Evolving Virus", Winter 1998, an article on what other diseases teach us about AIDS.

Publication:
OUT EXTRA:

Art Director:
JAMES CONRAD

Editor:
SARAH PETTIT

Publishing Company:
Out Publishing, Inc.

CHRISTOPHER ANNON
1 Sackett Street #3R
Brooklyn, NY 11231
8-875-7509

65

Illustration for "A Bitterness In the Air", June 1997, a review of the book 'Reading in the Dark', a story set in a depressed and divided 1950's Northern Ireland.

Publication:
THE BOSTON BOOK REVIEW

Art Director:
SUSAN ARNOTT

Designer:
SUSAN ARNOTT

Editor:
THEOHARIS CONSTANTINE THEOHARIS

Publishing Company:
The Boston Book Review, Ltd.

MICHELLE CHANG
3rd Street #4L
Brooklyn, NY 11234
8-797-4427

66

Self-promotional piece using characters from the television show 'NYPD Blue'.

67

Self-promotional piece of James Dean.

68

Self-promotional piece entitled 'Where All Pilots Go'.

R. GREGORY CHRISTIE
359 Jackson Avenue
Scotch Plains, NJ 07076
908-322-4280

65

Illustration for "About Face", March 1998, an article about the lifetime consequences of adolescent acne.

Publication:
LIVING FIT

Art Director:
LISA HATFIELD-LECONTE

Designer:
ANNIE HUANG

Publishing Company:
Weider Publications, Inc.

SEYMOUR CHWAST
The Pushpin Group
18 East 16th Street
New York, NY 10003
212-255-6456

70

Cover image for the special report "What Makes a Good School", October 27, 1997.

Publication:
TIME

Art Directors:
ARTHUR HOCHSTEIN AND CYNTHIA HOFFMAN

Designer:
ARTHUR HOCHSTEIN

Editor:
WALTER ISAACSON

Publishing Company:
Time Inc.

GREG CLARKE
214 Twin Falls Court
Thousand Oaks, CA 91320
805-499-8823
Rep.: Sally Heflin & The Artworks
212-366-1893

71

Illustration for a bagel company.

Client:
EINSTEIN BROS. BAGELS

Art Director:
STEVE SANDSTROM

Designer:
GREG CLARKE

Design Firm:
Sandstrom Design

CHRISTIAN CLAYTON
135 South La Brea Avenue #1
Los Angeles, CA 90036
213-936-8448

72

Portrait of Jimmie Rodgers entitled 'Thumbs Up on the Spot', for the article "The Singing Brakeman", October 1997.

Publication:
TEXAS MONTHLY

Art Director:
D.J. STOUT

Designer:
D.J. STOUT

Editor:
GREGORY CURTIS

Publishing Company:
Mediatex Communications

73

Illustration for the article "Suite for Ebony & Phonics", December 1997.

Publication:
DISCOVER

Art Director:
RICHARD BODDY

Designer:
RICHARD BODDY

Publishing Company:
Mediatex Communications

CHRISTIAN & ROB CLAYTON
See individual listings

74

Cover art for the Art Directors Club of Denver 'Call For Entries'.

Client:
ART DIRECTORS CLUB OF DENVER

Art Director:
LEE REEDY

Designer:
LEE REEDY

Design Firm:
Lee Reedy Creative

CHRISTIAN CLAYTON
See individual listing

75

Illustration for the article "Love", February 1998.

Publication:
SWING MAGAZINE

Art Director:
ELIZABETH AVEDON

Designer:
FRANCESCA PACCHINI

Editor:
DAVID LAUREN

ROB CLAYTON
4181/2 N. Orange Grove Avenue
Los Angeles, CA 90036
213-653-5192

76

Illustration for the artist's Christmas card, 1997.

77

'You Never Know When Sweet Turns to Sour'. (detail)

78-79

'Welcome Home'.

GARY CLEMENT
52 Arlington Avenue
Toronto, Ontario
M6G 3K8 Canada
416-657-8975

80

Illustration for an article on the sanctity of the "boys only" Friday night poker game, September 26, 1997.

Publication:
THE NEW YORK TIMES

Art Director:
LINDA BREWER

Publishing Company:
The New York Times Co.

81-82

One of two from a series of twelve for the "Letters to the Editors" column.

Publication:
REPORT ON BUSINESS MAGAZINE

Art Director:
KASPAR DELINE

Editor:
PATRICIA BEST

Publishing Company:
Thompson Newspapers

ALAN E. COBER
Deceased

83

Commissioned, yet unpublished piece entitled 'Plane Crash'.

Publication:
THE NEW YORKER

Illustration Director:
CHRIS CURRY

Publishing Company:
Condé Nast Publications, Inc.

TAVIS COBURN
350 East Delmar Boulevard #301
Pasedena, CA 91101
626-585-1716

84

Student editorial assignment about the disappearing middle class.

Professor:
JIM HEIMANN

85

Student editorial assignment on Mike Tyson.

Professor:
JIM HEIMANN

SUE COE
214 East 84th Street #3C
New York, NY 10028

86

Illustration for an article on the murder of rapper The Notorious B.I.G., April 17, 1997.

Publication:
ROLLING STONE

Art Director:
FRED WOODWARD

Publishing Company:
Wenner Media, Inc.

87

Illustration for the article "Jane vs. Jane", December 1997/ January 1998, which described the unique child custody battles that arise when lesbian couples with children break up.

Publication:
OUT MAGAZINE

Designer:
GEORGE KARABOTSOS

Editor:
SARAH PETTIT

Publishing Company:
Out Publishing

JIM COHEN
107 Miller Road
Hawthorn Woods, IL 60047
847-726-8979

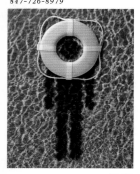

88-89

*One of two self-promotional pieces. **88** 'Kill the Ref'. **89** 'Lifesaver'.*

SANTIAGO COHEN
820 Park Avenue
Hoboken, NJ 07030
201-420-7275

90

Illustration for "Letting Go", April 28, 1997, which depicts the fear parents have when their children "fly solo".

Publication:
NEW YORK MAGAZINE

Art Director:
JENNIFER GILMAN

Designer:
ANDREA DUNHAM

Editor:
CAROLINE MILLER

Publishing Company:
Primedia, Inc.

JOHN COLLIER
1603 Wood Oak Drive
Richardson, TX 75082
972-238-9948

91

Portrait of slain rap artist The Notorious B.I.G. for a review of his posthumously released album 'Life After Death', May 1, 1997.

Publication:
ROLLING STONE

Art Director:
FRED WOODWARD

Publishing Company:
Wenner Media, Inc.

GENEVIÈVE CÔTÉ
400 De Maisonneuve West #851
Montréal Quebéc
H3A 1L4 Canada
514-282-9399

92

Illustration for the article "Dolly The Clone", May 1997.

Publication:
INTERFACE

Art Director:
DOMINIQUE MOUSSEAU

93

Illustration for the article "The Genetics of Women", December 1997.

Publication:
CLIN D'OEIL

Art Director:
PIERRE LEDUC

Publishing Company:
Publicor

BRIAN CRONIN
682 Broadway #4A
New York, NY 10012
212-254-6312

94

Illustration entitled 'Fat Face With Fork' which appeared on a poster for an exhibition of the artist's work at the Irish Museum of Modern Art.

95

Illustration for the article "Wenn Mütter Gehen...", June 1997.

Publication:
MARIE CLAIRE
(GERMANY)

Art Director:
GABRIEL ENGELS

Publishing Company:
Marie Claire

96

Portrait of David Bowie for "Sound +Fission", February 20, 1997, a review of his album 'Earthling'.

Publication:
ROLLING STONE

Art Director:
FRED WOODWARD

Publishing Company:
Wenner Media, Inc.

97

Illustration for "No Place To Heal", January/February 1998, an article on the use of healthcare halfway houses.

Publication:
HEALTH MAGAZINE

Art Director:
JANE PALECEK

Designers:
JANE PALECEK AND
STEVE POWELL

Publishing Company:
Time Inc.

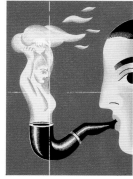

97

Illustration for the article "Make Love and War".

Publication:
ESQUIRE

Design Director:
ROBERT PRIEST

Art Director:
ROCKWELL HARWOOD

Publishing Company:
The Hearst Corporation

98

Personal piece.

99

Personal piece.

CSA ARCHIVE
TODD PIPER HAUSWIRTH AND
ERIK EMMINGS
30 North 1st Street
Minneapolis, MN 55401
612-339-5181

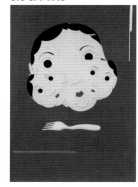

100

Illustration for a line of T-shirts.

Client:
CHUCK

Art Director:
TODD PIPER HAUSWIRTH

Design Firm:
CSA Archive

CSA ARCHIVE &
ERIK T. JOHNSON
See previous listing

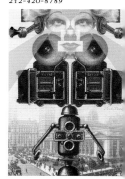

100

Illustration for a self-promotional postcard.

Art Director:
CHARLES S. ANDERSON

Design Firm:
CSA ARCHIVE

PAUL DALLAS
54 Rivercrest Road
Toronto, Ontario
M6S 4H3 Canada
416-762-3652

Illustration to promote a design firm; one from a series of images based on the illustrator's writing.

Client:
ZERO THRU 9 DESIGN
COMPANY INC.

Art Director:
JILL PETERS

MARK DANIELSO
914 North West 54th Street
Seattle, WA 98107-3647
206-789-2882

Self-promotional piece.

PAUL DAVIS
14 East 4th Street
New York, NY 10012
212-420-8789

Illustration for the article "Eye Tech", July 1997, an article on the future of technology and how video and audio are replacing books and literature.

Publication:
WORTH MAGAZINE

Art Director:
PHILIP BRATTER

Associate Art Director:
DEANNA LOWE

Editor:
JOHN KOTEN

Publishing Company:
Capitol Publishing

TER DE SÈVE
Park Place
oklyn, NY 11217
-398-8099

104

er for a novel about
Duke of Portland, an
tric hypochondriac who is
ly losing his mind, October
1997.

lication:
E UNDERGROUND
N

gner:
EANNE J. SERRA

lishing Company:
guin USA

105

er art entitled 'Through the
k, James', January 29, 1998.

lication:
E NEW YORKER

Editor:
ANÇOISE MOULY

lishing Company:
ndé Nast Publications, Inc.

106

er for a novel about a bear
takes a found manuscript to
York City and becomes a
ary sensation without it ever
g notice that he is a bear,
rch 1997.

lication:
E BEAR WENT OVER
E MOUNTAIN

Director:
Y KING

lishing Company:
ubleday Books

JEFFREY DECOSTER
3530a 22nd Street
San Francisco, CA 94114
415-206-9430
Rep.: Sally Heflin & The Artworks
212-366-1893

107

*Portrait of Johnny Depp for a
review of his movie 'Dead Man',
October 6, 1997.*

Publication:
THE NEW YORKER

Illustration Editor:
CHRIS CURRY

Publishing Company:
Condé Nast Publications, Inc.

ETIENNE DELESSERT
P.O. Box 1689
5 Lakeview Avenue
Lakeville, CT 06039

108

*Portrait of Philip of Spain for
the book review "The King Who
Sent the Armada", August 1997.*

Publication:
THE ATLANTIC
MONTHLY

Art Director:
JUDY GARLAN

Publishing Company:
The Atlantic Monthly

KIM DEMARCO
6 East 12th Street #3
New York, NY 10003
212-675-2023

109

*Illustration for an alternative
dance performance entitled 'Late
Night Sugar Flight' at P.S. 122,
for the "Goings on About Town"
section, July 12, 1998.*

Publication:
THE NEW YORKER

Associate Illustration Editor:
OWEN PHILLIPS

Publishing Company:
Condé Nast Publications, Inc.

ISABELLE DERVAUX
c/o Riley Illustration
155 West 15th Street
New York, NY 10011
212-989-8770

110

*Illustration entitled
'L'Etiquetage', for the shopper's
guide, 'Le Guide du Tout'.*

Art Director:
GILLES VALETTE

Designer:
GILLES VALETTE

Design Firm:
Nicolitch & Valette

Agency:
Alice

NICK DEWAR
c/o Kate Larkworthy
Artist Representation, Ltd.
32 Downing Street #4D
New York, NY 10014
212-633-1310

111

*Illustration for "Hold Me! Squeeze
Me! Buy Me a Six-Pack!",
November 16, 1997, an article on
branding one's own name.*

Publication:
THE NEW YORK TIMES
MAGAZINE

Art Director:
SAM REEP

Designer:
LISA NAFTOLIN

Editor:
TRIP GAABRIEL

Publishing Company:
The New York Times Co.

112

*illustration for the article "The 'I'
of the Storm", August 24, 1997.*

Publication:
THE NEW YORK TIMES
MAGAZINE

Art Director:
JANET FROELICH

Designer:
LISA NAFTOLIN

Publishing Company:
The New York Times Co.

HENRIK DRESCHER
c/o Reactor Art & Design
51 Camden Street
Toronto, Ontario
M5V 1V2 Canada
1-800-730-8945

113

*illustration for "Options Faux
Sale", July/August 1997, an
article on how to protect your
cheap stocks from a big tax bite.*

Publication:
BLOOMBERG
PERSONAL FINANCE

Art Director:
CAROL LAYTON

Designer:
FRANK TAGARIELLO

Editor:
WILLIAM H. INMAN

Publishing Company:
Bloomberg L.P.

GÉRARD DUBOIS
c/o Marlena Agency
278 Hamilton Avenue
Princeton, NJ 08540
609-252-9405

114

*Opening illustration for the article
"Juggling Large Message Stores",
July 1, 1997.*

Publication:
NETWORK COMPUTING

Art Director:
ATHENA VORILLAS

Designer:
ATHENA VORILLAS

Editor:
SUE IRSFELD

Publishing Company:
CMP Media

115

*Cover art for 'Si Noel Vous
Chante...', November 1997, a CD
with various artists performing
old Christmas songs.*

Client:
GESTION SON &
IMAGE/MUSICOR

Art Director:
MARIE-JOSÉE CHAGNON

Designer:
MARIE-JOSÉE CHAGNON

116

*Illustration of the dance piece
'33 Fainting Spells' from the show
'The Uninvited', for the "Goings
On About Town" section,
November 10, 1997.*

Publication:
THE NEW YORKER

Associate Illustration Editor:
OWEN PHILLIPS

Publishing Company:
Condé Nast Publications, Inc.

117

Book cover, June 1997

Publication:
LA VENGEANCE D'UN PÈRE

Art Director:
GÉRARD DUBOIS

Designer:
FRANCE LAFOND

Editor:
BRIGITTE BOUCHARD

Author:
PAN BOUYOUCAS

Publishing Company:
Libre Expression

118

Opening illustration for the article "A Guide to Managed Care", January 1998.

Publication:
MODERN MATURITY

Art Director:
CYNTHIA FRIEDMAN

Editor:
KAREN REYES

Writer:
SUSAN DENTZER

Publishing Company:
A.A.R.P.

119

Illustration for "Sounds From a Can", August 1997, an article on how to choose stock music.

Publication:
MACWORLD

Art Director:
SYLVIA CHEVRIER

Editor:
KATE ULRICH

Publishing Company:
Mac Publishing

THE DYNAMIC DUO STUDIO
95 Kings Highway South
Westport, CT 06880
203-454-4518

120-121

One of two illustrations which accompanied the published screenplay of the movie 'Scream', Spring 1997.

Publication:
SCENARIO MAGAZINE

Line Work:
ARLEN SCHUMER

Color:
SHERRI WOLFANG

Art Director:
ANDREW KNER

Editor:
TODD LIPPY

Publishing Company:
RC Publications

EDEM ELESH
806 North Gardner Street
Los Angeles, CA 90046
213-951-1083

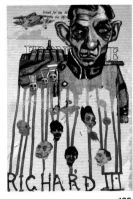

122

Theater poster for a production of 'Richard III'.

Client:
BUFFALO NIGHTS THEATRE COMPANY

Art Director:
M. KYLE HOLLINGSWORTH

Designer:
EDEM ELESH

Design Firm:
56 Design

IAN FALCONER
33 West 9th Street
New York, NY 10011

123

Cover illustration entitled 'Mother's Day', May 12, 1997.

Publication:
THE NEW YORKER

Art Editor:
FRANÇOISE MOULY

Publishing Company:
Condé Nast Publications, Inc.

INGO FAST
25 Broadway
Brooklyn, NY 11211
718-387-9570

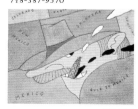

124-125

Personal piece entitled 'Texas'.

126

Personal piece entitled 'Trident and Halo' (Midtown at 2:00am).

IVETTA FEDOROVA
640 Broadway #3E
New York, NY 10012
212-673-5363

127

Illustration for the book review "Can't Steer from the Back Seat of Life", September 1997.

Publication:
THE NEW YORK TIMES BOOK REVIEW

Art Director:
STEVEN HELLER

Designer:
STEVEN HELLER

Editor:
CHARLES McGRATH

Publishing Company:
The New York Times Co.

JEFFREY FISHER
c/o Riley Illustration
155 West 15th Street
New York, NY 10011
212-989-8770

128

One from a series for a promotional calendar.

Client:
BAKER DESIGN ASSOCIATES

Art Director:
MICHELLE WOLINS

VIVIENNE FLESHER
415-921-2440

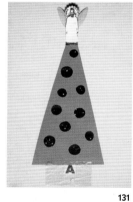

129

Illustration for the article "Ballet", February 1997.

Publication:
SAN FRANCISCO MAGAZINE

Art Director:
JORGE COLUMBO

Designer:
JORGE COLUMBO

EDWIN FOTHERINGHAM
5008 Baker Avenue NW
Seattle, WA 98107

130

Illustration for the article "Wicked Hitch Craft", March 28, 1997, a review of the newly restored Alfred Hitchcock film 'Vertigo'.

Publication:
ENTERTAINMENT WEEKLY

Design Director:
JOHN KORPICS

Designer:
GEORGE M. CALMAN

Publishing Company:
Time Inc.

130

Illustration for the article "Evolution of Style", September 1997.

Publication:
QUEST

Creative Director
MICHAEL GROSSMAN

Art Director:
JEFF CHRISTENSEN

Publishing Company:
Meigher Communications

LISA FRANKE
5208 3rd Avenue South
Minneapolis, MN 55419
612-824-6290

131

Illustration created for the studio Christmas card.

Design Firm:
FRANKE DESIGN

CRAIG FRAZIER
90 Throckmorton Avenue #28
Mill Valley, CA 94941
415-389-1475

130

Illustration for the article "Breast Cancer – What Every Woman Should Know", Summer 1997.

Publication:
"H"

Art Director:
ANDY DEARWATER

Designer:
ANDY DEARWATER

Design Firm:
DEARWATER DESIGN

Editor:
GABRIELLE COSGRIFF

Publishing Company:
Hermann Hospital's Dept. of Public Affairs & Marketing

Illustration for the article "Enterprising Nonprofits", January/February 1998

Publication:
HARVARD BUSINESS REVIEW

Art Director:
LANCE HIDY

Editor:
THOMAS KIELY

Publishing Company:
Harvard Business Review

ARK
EDRICKSON
8 East Rock Ridge Court
on, AZ 85749
-760-5667

134

er illustration for the feature
ow We Get Addicted",
y 5, 1997.

lication:
ME

Director:
HUR HOCHSTEIN

igner:
HUR HOCHSTEIN

or:
LTER ISAACSON

lishing Company:
e Inc.

135

stration of the character
oman from the television show
nfeld, May 30, 1997, that
with the quote from Jerry on
oman, "He's pure evil...He's
tery wrapped in a Twinkie"

lication:
TERTAINMENT
EKLY

ign Director:
HN KORPICS

Director
E KIMBERLING

igner:
E KIMBERLING

lishing Company:
e Inc.

DREW FRIEDMAN
68 Walker Lake
Shohola, PA 18458

136-137

*Illustration entitled "Seven
Arguments for Mass Transit",
December 22-29 1997,
commenting on the unpopular
celebrity voice-overs that are
heard in all NYC taxi cabs.*

Publication:
NEW YORK MAGAZINE

Design Director:
MARK MICHAELSON

Art Director:
FLORIAN BACHLEDA

Publishing Company:
Primedia, Inc.

THOMAS FUCHS
Stocken 26
73479 Ellwangen, Germany
011-49-7961-6832

138-141

*One of four selections from
a series of 101 based on 'Grimm's
Fairy Tales', August 1997.*

MARK GAGNON
460 West 24th Street #14D
New York, NY 10011
212-727-0266

142-143

*One of two from the fashion
story "Shock Around the Clock",
January 19, 1997.*

Publication:
THE NEW YORK TIMES
MAGAZINE

Art Director:
JANET FROELICH

Designer:
LISA NAFTOLIN

Publishing Company:
The New York Times Co.

MILTON GLASER
207 East 32nd Street
New York, NY 10016

144-145

Portrait of artist Francis Bacon.

Publication:
THE NEW YORK TIMES
BOOK REVIEW

Art Director:
STEVEN HELLER

Publishing Company:
The New York Times Co.

DAVID GOLDIN
111 Fourth Avenue
New York, NY 10003
212-529-5195

146

*Personal piece inspired by
the view out of the artist's window.*

147

*Illustration of cops, robbers
and lawyers for the article
"John Murphy's Law".*

Publication:
NORTHEAST

Art Director
PATTY COUSINS

Publishing Company:
The Hartford Courant
Sunday Magazine

EDWARD GOREY
P.O. Box 146
Yarmouthport, MA 02675

148

*One drawing from the story
"The Haunted Tea Cozy",
December 21, 1997.*

Publication:
THE NEW YORK TIMES
MAGAZINE

Art Director:
JANET FROELICH

Designer:
JOEL CUYLER

Publishing Company:
The New York Times Co.

JOSH GOSFIELD
200 Varick Street Ste. 508
New York, NY 10014

149

*Portrait of Malcom X's wife
Betty Shabazz, killed in a fire
set by her grandson, for the
"Spotlight" feature.*

Publication:
TIME

Art Director:
ARTHUR HOCHSTEIN

Designer:
JOE ASLAENDER

Editor:
WALTER ISSACSON

Publishing Company:
Time Inc.

ALEXA GRACE
530 West 236th Street #3G
Riverdale, NY 10463
718-884-6737
212-254-4424

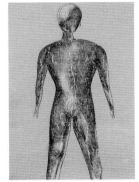

150

*Illustration for the article
"Under Pressure", Spring 1997.*

Publication:
STANFORD MEDICINE
MAGAZINE

Art Director:
DAVID ARMARIO

151

*Illustration for the article "The
New Miracle Drug", June 1997.*

Publication:
GLAMOUR

Art Director:
KATI KORPIJAAKKO

Publishing Company:
Condé Nast Publications, Inc.

GEOFFREY GRAHN
4054 Madison Avenue #E
Culver City, CA 90232
310-838-7824

152-153

*One of six frames from the
unproduced animated CD-ROM
"Forks and Sockets", where
children of the world experiment
with international sockets using
the local flatware.*

Client:
INSCAPE

Art Director:
REBEKAH BEHRENDT

152-153

*One of six frames from the
unproduced animated short
"Egg Salad" for the Museum of
Household Accidents.*

Client:
INSCAPE

Art Director:
REBEKAH BEHRENDT

154

*Portrait of Thom Yorke, lead
singer of the band Radiohead, as
their album was named album of
the year, Year-End Special 1997.*

Publication:
ENTERTAINMENT
WEEKLY

Design Director:
JOHN KORPICS

Art Director:
JOE KIMBERLING

Designer:
JOE KIMBERLING

Publishing Company:
Time Inc.

155

*Illustration for a list of personal
don'ts entitled "Don't Shave Your
Hydraulics", for the article "That
Thing You Do? Maybe You
Shouldn't. In fact, Just Don't",
September 1997.*

Publication:
ESQUIRE

Design Director:
ROBERT PRIEST

Art Director:
ROCKWELL HARWOOD

Publishing Company:
The Hearst Corporation

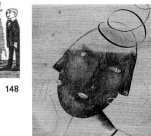

156

*Illustration for "Where Sin is
Taken Seriously", August 1997,
about the Devil's prevalence in
Southern politics and culture.*

Publication:
THE NEW YORK TIMES

Art Director:
NICHOLAS BLECHMAN

Editor:
KATY ROBERTS

Publishing Company:
The New York Times Co.

GREEN & READ
415 West 24th Street #5I
New York, NY 10011
212-929-6696

157

Portrait of musician Goldie for the review of his album 'Saturnz Return', February 5, 1998.

Publication:
ROLLING STONE

Art Director:
FRED WOODWARD

Deputy Art Director:
GAIL ANDERSON

Publishing Company:
Wenner Media, Inc

WILLIAM GRIFFITHS
43 Black Knight Road
St. Catharines, Ontario
L2N 3B9 Canada
905-937-4164

158

Student assignment to illustrate an ad for a guitar magazine, entitled 'Soul Therapy'.

ROBERT GROSSMAN
19 Crosby Street
New York, NY 10013
212-925-1965 Tel.
212-925-2001 Fax.

6-7

Juror portrait, Nicholas Blechman

STEVEN GUARNACCIA
31 Fairfield Street
Montclair, NJ 07042
973-746-9785

159

Illustration for "Sleeping with the Enemy", June 1996, an article about the hazards of being in a relationship with someone in a competing work situation.

Publication:
FAST COMPANY

Art Director:
GRETCHEN SMELTER

Publishing Company:
U.S. News & World Report/The Atlantic Monthly

160

Illustration for "Executioner", an article which opposed the use of the death penalty, October 1997.

Publication:
NESSUNO TOCCHI CAINO

Art Directors:
FAUSTA ORECCHIO AND ROSA SCHIAVELLO

Publishing Company:
Associanzione Maria Teressa Di Lascia

161

Swatch Watch called 'Roboboy' extolling the virtues of analog vs digital timekeeping.

Client:
SWATCH

Art Director:
CARLO GIORDANETTI

Designer:
STEVEN GUARNACCIA

AMY GUIP
91 East 4th Street 6th Floor
New York, NY 10003

162-163

Illustration for "Chasing Barbie", a story on plastic surgery, March 2, 1998.

Publication:
JUMP MAGAZINE

Art Director:
CHRYSTAL FALCIONI

Designer:
CHRYSTAL FALCIONI

Editor:
LORI BERGER

Publishing Company:
Weider Publications, Inc.

EDMUND GUY
309 Race Track Road
Hohokus, NJ 07423
201-251-7660

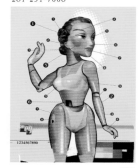

164

Illustration indicating potential surgery procedures on an idealised figure, for the article "Plastic Surgery", Spring 1997.

Publication:
CAROLINAS HEALTH CARE SYSTEM

Art Director:
BRENT MILLER

Designer:
BRENT MILLER

Publishing Company:
Medical Life Publishing

165

Portrait of Prodigy's' Keith Flint for "Top of the Fops", July 11, 1997, about three British bands.

Publication:
ENTERTAINMENT WEEKLY

Design Director:
JOHN KORPICS

Art Director:
MICHAEL PICÓN

Publishing Company:
Time Inc.

166

Portrait of Roseanne as her television series ended, for the article "And Away She Goes", May 2, 1997.

Publication:
ENTERTAINMENT WEEKLY

Design Director:
JOHN KORPICS

Art Director:
MICHAEL PICÓN

Publishing Company:
Time Inc.

MICK HAGGERTY
c/o BRAINS
mick@brainsite.com

Cover illustration.

ERIC HANSON
4444 Upton Avenue South
Minneapolis, MN 55410
612-927-9054

167

Self-promotional piece diagramming the emotion, 'Shadenfreude.'

JESSIE HARTLAND
165 William Street
New York, NY 10038
212-233-1413

168

Illustration showing different jean styles, for a promotional mailer.

Client:
LEVI STRAUSS & CO.

Creative Director:
PAUL HUBER

Art Director:
GRACE MELLOW

Design Firm:
Miller/Huber Relationship Marketing

VIRGINIA HATLEY
131 Fifth Avenue #304
New York, NY 10003

169

Illustration for "Shrink Rap/ Rude Questions" a Q&A with psychotherapists, November 1997.

Publication:
GQ

Art Director:
JOHN BOYER

Publishing Company:
Condé Nast Publications, Inc.

MARTYN HEILIG
38941 Bella Vista Road
Temucula, CA 92592
909-699-8625

170

Portrait of Robert Downey Jr., part of a school assignment, December 1997.

Art Director:
JASON HOLLEY

SANDRA HENDLE
1823 Spruce Street
Philadelphia, PA 19103
215-735-7380

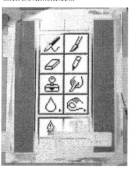

Illustration for a book about a troupe of "very special people".

Art Director:
SANDRA HENDLER

Designer:
SANDRA HENDLER

JOYCE HESSELBERTH
c/o Spur
3647 Falls Road
Baltimore, MD 21211
410-235-7803

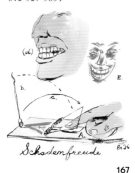

Cover illustration for the featur "Waste Reduction Emphasis", August 1997.

Publication:
WASTE AGE MAGAZIN

Art Director:
KIMBERLY LEAIRD

Designer:
KIMBERLY LEAIRD

Editor:
JOHN AQUINO

Publishing Company:
Environmental Industry Association

JODY HEWGILL
260 Brunswick Avenue
Toronto, Ontario
M5S 2M7 Canada
416-924-4200
Rep: Sally Heflin & The Artwo
212-366-1893

Portrait for the ad campaign "Clopixol and Fluanxol-For th Many Faces of Schizophrenia"

Client:
LUNDBECK

Designer:
STEPHANIE BEAUGRAND

Design Firm:
Graphème Inc.

AL HIRSCHFELD

Margo Feiden Galleries Ltd.
Madison Avenue
New York, NY 10021

174

Portrait of film director Steven Spielberg for the 'Power 101' issue, October 31, 1997.
Publication:
ENTERTAINMENT WEEKLY
Design Director:
JOHN KORPICS
Art Director:
GERALDINE HESSLER
Publishing Company:
Time Inc.

175

Portrait of Clare Booth-Luce for a story on the editor/writer, May 26, 1997.
Publication:
THE NEW YORKER
Illustration Editor:
CHRIS CURRY
Publishing Company:
Condé Nast Publications, Inc.

PAMELA HOBBS

www.Pamorama.com
pay4u@aol.com

176

Cover illustration for a music guide.
Client:
WARNER BROS.
Art Director:
MICHAEL DIEHL
Design Firm:
Michael Diehl Design

PETER HOEY

c/o Gerald & Cullen Rapp
108 East 35th Street
New York, NY 10016
212-889-3337
www.peterhoey.com

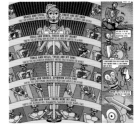

177

One from the story "Valse Mecanique", Fall 1997.
Publication:
BLAB! #9
Art Director:
MONTE BEAUCHAMP
Designer:
MONTE BEAUCHAMP
Editor:
MONTE BEAUCHAMP
Publishing Company:
Fantagraphics

BRAD HOLLAND

96 Greene Street
New York, NY 10012
212-226-3675

178-179

One of two illustrations from a series for the feature "Confessions of a Short-Order Artist", May 1997.
Publication:
PERSÖNLICH
Art Director:
BRAD HOLLAND
Designer:
BRAD HOLLAND
Editor:
OLIVER PRANGE
Publishing Company:
Persönlich Verlags AG

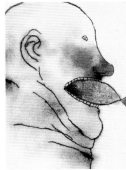

180-181

One of two illustrations from a series of chapter title pages.
Publication:
THE ART DIRECTORS CLUB OF SWITZERLAND ANNUAL 1997
Art Directors:
ROLAND SCOTONI AND BRAD HOLLAND
Designer:
ROLAND SCOTONI
President:
HELEN MÜLLER

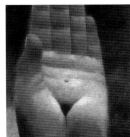

182

Illustration for the article "The Coming Crisis – In the new literature of love, orgasms are increasingly solo contendere", September 1997.
Publication:
ESQUIRE
Design Director:
ROBERT PRIEST
Art Director:
ROCKWELL HARWOOD
Editor:
RANDY ROTHENBERG
Publishing Company:
The Hearst Corporation

JASON HOLLEY

852 Monterey Road
South Pasedena, CA 91030
626-403-0152

183

Illustration for the feature "Long Gone-A Mystery Without End", December 1997, about Amy Bechtel, a runner who vanished in the mountains of Wyoming.
Publication:
OUTSIDE MAGAZINE
Art Director:
DAVE ALLEN
Publishing Company:
Mariah Media Inc.

184

Illustration for an annual report.
Client:
AUTOCAM
Art Director:
LESLIE BLACK
Design Firm:
Leslie Black

185

Illustration for "It Takes Guts", October 1996, an excerpt from 'Play in Traffic', a book about the Mütter Museum at the College of Physicians of Philadelphia.
Publication:
TRAVEL & LEISURE
Art Director:
VALLORIE FONG
Publishing Company:
American Express

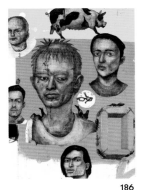

186

Illustration of the band Radiohead for a review of their album 'OK Computer', July 10-24, 1997.
Publication:
ROLLING STONE
Art Director:
FRED WOODWARD
Deputy Art Director:
GAIL ANDERSON
Publishing Company:
Wenner Media, Inc.

187

Illustration for the album 'Hydrangea' by Kate Jacobs.
Client:
BAR NONE RECORDS
Art Director:
LISA WAGNER
Design Firm:
Harpy Inc.

M. KYLE HOLLINGSWORTH

806 North Gardner Street
Los Angeles, CA 90046
213-951-1083

188

Poster for a production of 'Tristessa'.
Client:
BUFFALO NIGHTS THEATRE COMPANY
Art Director:
EDEM ELESH
Designer:
M. Kyle Hollingsworth
Design Firm:
56 Design

HADLEY HOOPER

2111 West 31st Avenue
Denver, CO 80211
303-458-6077

189

Portrait of George Grosz.

JOHN H. HOWARD

115 West 23rd Street #43A
New York, NY 10011
212-260-6700

190

Illustration for the article "The Loves We Leave Behind", April 1998
Publication:
READERS DIGEST
Art Directors:
JAMES McMULLAN AND HANNAU LAAKSO
Publishing Company:
The Readers Digest Assoc.

DAVID HUGHES

43 Station Road
Marple, Cheshire
SK66AJ England

191

Director James Cameron with Leonardo DiCaprio for "Magnificent Obsession", December 1997, an article about the making of the movie 'Titanic'.
Publication:
PREMIERE
Art Director:
DAVID MATT
Designer:
DAVID MATT
Editor:
ANNE THOMPSON
Publishing Company:
Hachette Filipacchi

192

Illustration for the feature "Rock of the Aged – The Giants of a Generation Roll into the Autumn of Their Musical Lives", October 3, 1997.
Publication:
ENTERTAINMENT WEEKLY
Design Director:
JOHN KORPICS
Designer:
DIRK BARNETT
Publishing Company:
Time Inc.

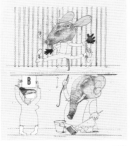

193

Illustration for the commentary "On the Role of Upholstery in Cardiovascular Physiology", November 1997.
Publication:
DISCOVER MAGAZINE
Art Director:
RICHARD BODDY
Designer:
RICHARD BODDY
Editor:
MARC ZABLUDOFF
Publishing Company:
Disney Publishing

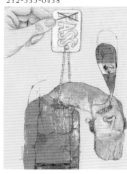

194

Publication:
THE NEW YORKER

Illustration Editor:
CHRIS CURRY

Publishing Company:
Condé Nast Publications, Inc.

HUNGRY DOG STUDIO
1361 Markan Court #3
Atlanta, GA 30306
404-872-7496

197

Portrait of actor Brad Pitt depicting some of the darker roles he has played.

Publication:
BRAD PITT

Art Director:
RICHARD BAKER

Designer:
RICHARD BAKER

Editor:
HOLLY GEORGE-WARREN

Publishing Company:
Little/Brown

TIM HUSSEY
231 East 76th Street #5D
New York, NY 10021
212-535-0438

200

Illustration which depicts revenge on a cocky snowboarding competition judge.

Publication:
TRANSWORLD
SNOWBOARDING

Art Directors:
JOE MITCH

Publishing Company:
Transworld Media

JORDIN ISIP
536 5th Street #2
Brooklyn, NY 11215
718-499-0985

204

Cover image celebrating the Centennial of the Declaration of Philippine Independence, the upcoming Presidential elections and the new millennium.

Publication:
PHILIPPINES YEARBOOK
1998 EDITION

Art Director:
VERNON GO

Designer:
ELMER BACASMAS

Editor:
VERNON GO

Publishing Company:
The Fookien Times
Yearbook Publishing Co.

JOEL PETER JOHNSON
P.O. Box 3642
Houston, TX 77253-3642
713-223-0373

207

Poster art for the AIGA 50 Covers/50 Books show, 1996.

Client:
AIGA

Art Directors:
JESSICA HELFAND AND
WILLIAM DRENTTEL

Designer:
JEFFREY D. TYSON

Design Firm:
Jessica Helfand/
William Drenttel

WILLIAM JOYCE
3302 Centenary Boulevard
Shreveport, LA 71104

Opening illustration entitled 'The Wizard', for the 'Power 100' issue, October 31, 1997.

Publication:
ENTERTAINMENT
WEEKLY

Design Director:
JOHN KORPICS

Art Director:
GERALDINE HESSLER

Designer:
GERALDINE HESSLER

Publishing Company:
Time Inc.

PHIL HULING
938 Bloomfield Street
Hoboken, NJ 07030
201-795-9366

195

Illustration for the feature "Cold Mountain" naming Charles Frazier's book of the same name 'Book of the Year', Year-End Special issue, 1997.

Publication:
ENTERTAINMENT
WEEKLY

Design Director:
JOHN KORPICS

Art Director:
JOE KIMBERLING

Designer:
JOE KIMBERLING

Publishing Company:
Time Inc.

196

Portrait of Martha Stewart for "A Good Thing?", July 4, 1997, a review of her book 'Martha Stewart – Just Desserts'.

Publication:
ENTERTAINMENT
WEEKLY

Design Director:
JOHN KORPICS

Art Director:
DIRK BARNETT

Publishing Company
Time Inc.

198

Portrait of Saddam Hussein and the many faces he wears, for the "Notebook" feature, November 24, 1997.

Publication:
TIME

Art Directors:
ARTHUR HOCHSTEIN AND
KENNETH SMITH

Publishing Company:
Time Inc

199

Portrait of Trey Anastasio of the rock group Phish, for the 'Table of Contents' page February 20, 1997.

Publication:
ROLLING STONE

Art Directors:
FRED WOODWARD AND
GERALDINE HESSLER

Publishing Company:
Wenner Media, Inc.

MIRKO ILIĆ
207 East 32nd Street
New York, NY 10016
212-481-9737

201

Visual pun playing off the title 'Cultural Roots', for a calendar entitled 'Speak to us of Children', October 1997.

Art Director:
MICHAEL CONNELL

Publishing Company:
Media Artists Inc. SRL

201

Illustration using DNA and Infinity symbols, for the article "Ewe Two", December 1997, about the first cloning of sheep.

Publication:
THE NEW YORK TIMES
BOOK REVIEW

Art Director:
STEVEN HELLER

Publishing Company:
The New York Times Co.

KEI ISHIHARA
33 Gold Street #1A
New York, NY 10038
212-964-9895

202-203

Self-promotional piece.

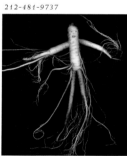

205

Promotional piece entitled 'Rice God', illustrating the song '50%' by the band Splashdown, for the benefit CD 'Nigh'.

Art Director:
CYNTHIA VON BUHLER

Design Firm:
Stoltze Design

ERIK T. JOHNSON
230 Oak Grove Street #626
Minneapolis, MN 55403
612-871-2907

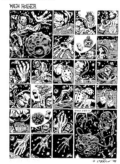

206

Illustration commissioned by Urban Outfitters and then used as a self-promotional poster

Publication:
SLANT MAGAZINE

Art Director:
HOWARD BROWN

Designer:
ERIK T. JOHNSON

208-209

TED JOUFLAS
303 West Olympic Place #301
Seattle, WA 98119
206-282-9803

One of three in a series of illustrations from a graphic novel, May 1997.

Publication:
SCARY!

Art Director:
TED JOUFLAS

Designer:
TED JOUFLAS

Editor:
ARY GROTH

Publishing Company:
Fantagraphics Books

GARY KELLEY
301 1/2 Main Street
Cedar Falls, IA 50613
319-277-2330

One from a series of images illustrating the screenplay 'All About Eve', Fall 1997.

Publication:
SCENARIO MAGAZINE

Art Director:
ANDREW KNER

Editor:
TOD LIPPY

Publishing Company:
RC Publications, Inc.

Portrait of Al Pacino depicting his roles in the three 'Godfather' films, for the article "Triple Face" May 2, 1997.

Publication:
ENTERTAINMENT
WEEKLY

Design Director:
JOHN KORPICS

Designer:
ALISHA DRUCKS

Publishing Company:
Time Inc.

ICHAEL KLEIN
Edgewood Road
dison, NJ 07940
-765-0623

213

stration for the article
r. Right", July 21, 1997,
ebate on what men really
t in men's magazines.
Publication:
W YORK MAGAZINE
t Director:
RIAN BACHLEDA
signer:
NDREA DUNHAM
tor-In-Chief:
AROLINE MILLER
blishing Company:
media, Inc.

OBERT KOPECKY
26 West 2nd Street
npe, AZ 85281

214

stration for the article
rime – Nirvana in the Can",
ne 27, 1997.
blication:
HE NEW YORK TIMES
AGAZINE
t Director:
ANET FROELICH
esigner:
AUL JEAN
blishing Company:
e New York Times Co.

TRISHA KRAUSS
277 West 11th Street #2C
New York, NY 10014
212-243-5975

215-217

One of three from a series
for the article "Technology with a
Human Face", December 7, 1997,
illustrating holiday gift ideas.
Publication:
THE WASHINGTON
POST MAGAZINE
Art Director:
KELLY DOE
Designer:
KELLY DOE
Editor:
SUSANNA GARDINER
Publishing Company:
The Washington Post Co.

ANJA KROENCKE
c/o Kate Larkworthy Artist
Representation, Ltd.
32 Downing Street #4D
New York, NY 10014
212-633-1310

218

Illustration for the fashion story
"Night and Day", Spring 1998.
Publication:
THE NEW YORK TIMES
FASHIONS OF
THE TIMES
Art Directors:
MICHAEL ROCK AND
GEORGIE STOUT
Designers:
MICHAEL ROCK AND
GEORGIE STOUT
Editor:
HOLLY BRUBACK
Publishing Company:
The New York Times Co.

219

Illustration for the article
"The Power of Personal Style",
Spring 1998.
Publication:
WOMAN'S DAY BEAUTY
Art Director:
VICTORIA MADDOCKS
Designers:
VICTORIA MADDOCKS AND
SANDRA MONTEPARO
Editor:
MARY LISA GAVENAS
Publishing Company:
Hachette Filipacchi

STEPHEN KRONINGER
303 Mercer #B304
New York, NY 10003
212-505-9150

220-221

One from a series of key
frames from the video 'Bad Phone
Sex' with Chris Rock.
Client:
HBO DOWNTOWN
Art Director:
STEPHEN KRONINGER
Designer:
STEPHEN KRONINGER
Animators:
PHILIP HOUGH,
KATHRYN BURKE AND
HOWARD HOFFMAN
Producer:
HOWARD HOFFMAN
Production Company:
Broadway Video

JULIA KUHL
217 East 29th Street #6I
New York, NY 10001
212-686-8684

222

Portrait to announce a
production of 'Uncle Tom's Cabin'
December 22, 1997.
Publication:
THE NEW YORKER
Deputy Illustration Editor:
OWEN PHILLIPS
Publishing Company:
Condé Nast Publications, Inc.

ANITA KUNZ
230 Ontario Street
Toronto, Ontario
M5A 2V5 Canada
416-364-3846

223

Illustration entitled 'Infanticide',
for the article "Why They Kill
Their Newborns", November 2,
1997, a history of infant deaths.
Publication:
THE NEW YORK TIMES
MAGAZINE
Art Director:
CATHY GILMORE-BARNES
Publishing Company:
The New York Times Co.

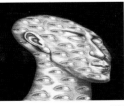

224

Portrait of Kramer from TV's
'Seinfeld', for the article
"The Seinfeld Chronicles",
May 30, 1997.
Publication:
ENTERTAINMENT
WEEKLY
Design Director:
JOHN KORPICS
Art Director:
JOE KIMBERLING
Publishing Company:
Time Inc.

225

Illustration of the band Cornershop,
for the 'Table of Contents' page,
October 30, 1997.
Publication:
ROLLING STONE
Art Director:
FRED WOODWARD
Deputy Art Director:
GAIL ANDERSON
Designer:
GAIL ANDERSON
Publishing Company:
Wenner Media, Inc.

226

Portrait of Medusa for an
insurance company advertisement.
Copyline: "For years we've faced
Marine liability risks other
companies turn away from".
Client:
MUTUAL MARINE
Art Director:
FRANK BARROWS
Designer:
FRANK BARROWS
Agency:
Creative Insurance
Marketing Company

227

Illustration entitled 'Intuition'.
Publication:
DAVID CARSON:
2ND SIGHT
Art Director:
DAVID CARSON
Editor:
LEWIS BLACKWELL
Publishing Company:
Universe Publishing/Rizzoli

227

One from a series for a
South African ad campaign.
Copyline: "Freudian Slip".
Client:
HOFBRAU BEER
Art Director:
ANTONELLA CAPOLILLO
Designer:
ANTONELLA CAPOLILLO
Agency:
The Jupiter Drawing Room

PETER KUPER
235 West 102nd Street #16U
New York, NY 10025
212-932-1722

228

Cover illustration for "Ready,
Fire, Aim", August 15, 1997,
a feature on the NRA.
Publication:
WASHINGTON CITY
PAPER
Art Director:
JANDOS ROTHSTEIN
Editor:
DAVID CARR
Publishing Company:
Thomas K. Yoder

229

One from a series for "Saved By
The Pill", November 24, 1997,
an article about the affect of
prescription drugs on children.
Publication:
NEW YORK MAGAZINE
Design Director:
MARK MICHAELSON
Designer:
JENNIFER GILMAN
Editor:
GEORGE KALOGERAKIS
Publishing Company:
Primedia, Inc.

230-231

One of three from a series for the feature "Burning Man", November 1997, that documented an annual event in the Nevada Desert of the same name.

Publication:
DETAILS

Design Director:
ROBERT NEWMAN

Designer:
ZOË MILLER

Editor:
ART SPIEGELMAN

Publishing Company:
Condé Nast Publications, Inc.

231

Illustration for "The First Amendment is not a Stop Sign Against Reform", December 1997, an article about campaign financing.

Publication:
THE PROGRESSIVE

Art Director:
PATRICK J.B. FLYNN

Editor:
MATTHEW ROTHSCHILD

Publishing Company:
The Progressive, Inc.

PHILIPPE LARDY
225 Lafayette Street #613
New York, NY 10012
212-473-3057

232-233

Detail from an article about alternative medicines entitled "The Best Medicine", October 1997.

Publication:
SHAPE MAGAZINE

Art Director:
YVONNE DURAN

Editor:
NANCY GOTTESMANN

Publishing Company:
Weider Publications, Inc.

234-235

Personal piece entitled 'La Transfiguraione'.

236

Illustration for an article about self-centered writers.

Publication:
GQ

Art Director:
JOHN BOYER

Publishing Company:
Condé Nast Publications, Inc.

237

Illustration for the article "Crossing Over to Motherhood".

Publication:
STANFORD MEDICINE MAGAZINE

Art Director:
PAUL CARSTENSEN

Publishing Company:
Stanford University

238

Illustration for the article "Italian Abolitionist Initiative at the U.N.", May 1997, which spoke against the use of the death penalty.

Publication:
HANDS OF CAIN

Art Director:
FAUSTA ORECCHIO

SCOTT LAUMANN
1820 Fulton Street #1
San Francisco, CA 94117
415-221-6496

239

Cover portrait of Lee Morgan, November 1997.

Publication:
GAVIN MAGAZINE

Art Director:
PETER GRAME

Publishing Company:
Miller Freeman Entertainment Group

ZOHAR LAZAR
c/o Kate Larkworthy Artist Representation, Ltd.
32 Downing Street #4D
New York, NY 10014
212-633-1310

240

Personal piece entitled 'The Cake Lady'.

241

Personal piece entitled 'Broad-Minded'.

242

Personal piece entitled 'The Crush'.

243

Portrait of Audie Murphy for the article "Last Page: Audie Murphy", November 1997.

Publication:
TEXAS MONTHLY

Art Directors:
D.J. STOUT AND NANCY MCMILLEN

Designer:
D.J. STOUT

Editor:
GREGORY CURTIS

Publishing Company:
Mediatex Communications

PIERRE LE-TAN
c/o Riley Illustration
155 West 15th Street
New York, NY 10011
212-989-8770

244

Portrait for the feature "A Fast Full Life, The Exceptional Legacy of H.H. Richardson".

Publication:
THE NEW YORKER

Illustration Editor:
CHRIS CURRY

Publishing Company:
Condé Nast Publications, Inc.

LAURA LEVINE
444 Broome Street
New York, NY 10013
212-431-4787

245

Two entitled 'Shipwreck' and 'Symphony of Sorrow' from a personal series on the Titanic.

KANDY LITTRELL
419 East 9th Street #4
New York, NY 10009
212-505-6036

246

Untitled personal piece.

ROSS MACDONALD
56 Castle Meadow Road
Newtown, CT 06470
203-270-6438

247

Illustration for "Flavor Faves", March 28, 1997, a feature on ten celebrity chefs.

Publication:
ENTERTAINMENT WEEKLY

Design Director:
JOHN KORPICS

Publishing Company:
Time Inc.

248

Illustration for "Windows 95 Headaches", an article on the frustrations with the software.

Publication:
PC WORLD

Art Director:
ROBERT KANES

Designer:
KATE GODFREY

Editor:
DANIEL TYNAN

Publishing Company:
PC World Magazine

Hand printed self-promotional piece.

Design Firm:
Brightwork Press

250-

Cover illustration for an annual report entitled "We are Prepared to Guide You", 1997.

Client:
NETWORK GENERAL

Art Director:
BILL CAHAN

Designer:
SHARRIE BROOKS

Design Firm:
Cahan & Associates

Opening illustration for the feature "Holiday Movie Preview", November 11, 1997.

Publication:
ENTERTAINMENT WEEKLY

Design Director:
JOHN KORPICS

Art Director:
JOE KIMBERLING

Designer:
JOE KIMBERLING

Publishing Company:
Time Inc.

ANK MADDOCKS
Market Street #4
ce, CA 90291
-396-4551

253

stration used for corporate
tity, promotion, posters,
ertisements and on CDs.

nt:
PITOL RECORDS

Director:
ss PATRICK

igner:
NK MADDOCKS

ign Firm:
t

EPHEN
ARQUART
Sharon Avenue
chanicsburg, PA 17055-6631
-766-3569

254

ne from a personal series
itled 'Numeropolis'.

AMES MARSH
Elms Road
ndon SW4 9ER U.K.
171 622 9530

255

ne in a series of six illustrations
an annual report entitled
teractivity'. Copyline: "Focusing
the Customer is Essential".

ient:
RION CAPITAL CORP.

t Director:
HRIS PASSEHL

esigner:
AMES MARSH

esign Firm:
assehl Design

RUTH MARTEN
8 West 13th Street #7RW
New york, NY 10011
212-645-0233

256

Unpublished cover depicting the
different hairstyles of New York.

Publication:
THE NEW YORKER

Art Editor:
FRANÇOISE MOULY

MATTHEW MARTIN
19 Prince Street #4
New York, NY 10012-3575
212-431-5033

257

Illustration for "Doing It by the
Book", June 23, 1997, a satirical
"memo" from the Department of
Defense. Re: Adultery.

Publication:
TIME

Art Director:
JOE ASLAENDER

Publishing Company:
Time Inc.

ADAM McCAULEY
2400 8th Avenue
Oakland, CA 94606

258

Illustration for an essay on
tourism and terrorism in the
Middle East entitled "Holy Terror.
A Middle Eastern Vocation",
December 16, 1997.

Publication:
THE VILLAGE VOICE

Art Director:
MINH UONG

Designer:
NICOLE SZYMANSKI

Publishing Company:
VV Publishing Corp.

259

Commissioned, yet unpublished
piece for an essay on the rise of
home theaters in the U.S.

Publication:
ARCHITECTURAL DIGEST
GERMAN EDITION

DAVID MAZZUCCELLI
123 West 93rd Street #8H
New York, NY 10025
212-666-7050

260

Portrait of Raskolnikov for
the article "Dostoyevsky's
Unabomber", February, 24, 1997.

Publication:
THE NEW YORKER

Illustration Editor:
CHRIS CURRY

Publishing Company:
Condé Nast Publications, Inc.

ADAM McCAULEY
2400 8th Avenue
Oakland, CA 94606

261

Opening illustration for the
feature "The Oscar Night
Prizefight", March 21, 1997.

Publication:
ENTERTAINMENT
WEEKLY

Associate Art Director:
JOHN WALKER

Designer:
JOHN WALKER

Publishing Company:
Time Inc.

262

Page from a personal travel
sketchbook kept on a trip to Egypt
illustrating Stella beer.

CHESLEY McCLAREN
125 West 79th Street
New York, NY 10024
212-496-1505

263

Promotional piece for a Spring
1998 Collection.

DAVID McLIMANS
c/o Gerald & Cullen Rapp
108 East 35th Street
New York, NY 10016
212-889-3337

264

Cover illustration for the travel
feature "Collage of Island
Choices", October 26, 1997.

Publication:
THE NEW YORK TIMES
TRAVEL SECTION

Art Director:
NICKIE KALISH

Designer:
SKIP JOHNSTON

Editor:
NANCY NEWHOUSE

Publishing Company:
The New York Times Co.

JAMES McMULLAN
207 East 32nd Street
New York, NY 10016
212-689-5527

265-267

One from a series of three
theater posters.

Client:
LINCOLN CENTER
THEATER

Executive Producer
BERNARD GERSTEN

Agency:
Russek Advertising

BROOKE MEINHARDT
375 Degraw Street 3rd Floor
Brooklyn, NY 11231
718-643-2726

6-7

Juror portrait, Geraldine Hessler.

SCOTT MENCHIN
AND IVETTA
FEDOROVA
See individual listings

268-269

Personal piece.

SCOTT MENCHIN
640 Broadway
New York, NY 10012
212-673-5363

270

Cover for the feature "The New
Retirement" February 16, 1997,
describing those over 65 who stay
vital with new careers or hobbies.

Publication:
THE BOSTON GLOBE
MAGAZINE

Art Director:
CATHERINE ALDRICH

Publishing Company:
The Boston Globe

DAVID MILLER
246 West 4th Street #3
New York, NY 10014
212-206-1265

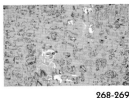

271

Cover for a novel by Milan
Kundera, January 1997.

Publication:
THE ART OF THE
NOVEL

Art Director:
JUSTUS OEHLER

Designer:
KRISTINA LANGHEIN

Publishing Company:
Faber & Faber

JOE MORSE

217 Indian Grove
Toronto, Ontario
M6P 2H4 Canada
416-516-2835
Rep: Sally Heflin & The Artworks
212-366-1893

272

One of four posters entitled "Show the World the Bottom of Your Shoes!" executed to promote Summer Hoops '97 in Italy, France and Sweden.

Client:
NIKE EUROPE

Art Director:
ERIK KESSELS

Designer:
ERIK HESEN

Print Producer:
PIETER LEENDERTSE

Agency:
Kesselskramer

273

Illustration for "In Search of a Black Eden", February 7, 1997, a review of the novel 'Paradise'.

Publication:
THE GLOBE AND MAIL

Art Director:
GUDRUN GALLO

Publishing Company:
Thompson Newspapers

274

Portrait of the Detroit Pistons' Grant Hill for an unused billboard campaign.

Art Director:
MARCELLE KNITTEL

JOEL NAKAMURA

72 Bobcat Trail
Santa Fe, NM 87505

275

Illustration for "It Coulda Happened – A Revised Nonlinear History", January 1997, which reviewed the advances of the past so to better plan for the future.

Publication:
MIX MAGAZINE

Art Director:
KAY MARSHALL

Publishing Company:
Cardinal Business Media

CHRISTOPH NIEMANN

Georg-Kropp Strasse 9
71638 Ludwigsburg Germany
chniemann@aol.com

276

Portrait of hip-hop artist Master P for the 'Table of Contents' page, November 27, 1997.

Publication:
ROLLING STONE

Art Director:
FRED WOODWARD

Publishing Company:
Wenner Media, Inc.

277

Illustration for the article "Adultery's Double Standard", October 12, 1997.

Publication:
THE NEW YORK TIMES MAGAZINE

Art Director:
JANET FROELICH

Publishing Company:
The New York Times Co.

278

Series from an upcoming book.

Publication:
THE GOOD PORTRAIT

Publishing Company:
Maro Verlag, Augsburg

CHRISTIAN NORTHEAST

336 Rusholme Road, Upper Floor
Toronto, Ontario
M6H 2Z5 Canada
416-538-0400

279

Self-promotional piece.

280

Illustration for "Free to Spend the Night", August 1997, a story about a slave who escaped to Canada via the underground railroad.

Publication:
TORONTO LIFE MAGAZINE

Art Director:
SANDRA LATIN

Publishing Company:
Toronto Life

281

Illustration used as promotion and corporate identity for a production company.

Client:
BLINK

Art Director:
DANA SAMUEL

Designer:
DANA SAMUEL

Design Firm:
Concrete Design

282

Self-promotional piece.

283

Self-promotional piece.

284

CD cover and poster for the Refreshments' album 'The Bottle and Fresh Horses'.

Client:
MERCURY RECORDS

Art Director:
JEFF SCHULTZ

Designer:
JEFF SCHULTZ

Design Firm:
Mercury Records

TIM O'BRIEN

Rep.: 212-953-7088

285

Portrait of former deputy chief of staff Harold Ickes with the Clinton campaign fund raising paper trail, April 14, 1997.

Publication:
TIME

Art Directors:
ARTHUR HOCHSTEIN AND KENNETH SMITH

Designer:
KENNETH SMITH

Editor:
WALTER ISAACSON

Publishing Company:
Time Inc.

FILIP PAGOWSKI

113 West 106th Street #4B
New York, NY 10025
212-665-7553

286

Ludwig Erhard, West Germany's first economics minister for the article "Loving the Mark", April 28-May 5, 1997.

Publication:
THE NEW YORKER

Illustration Director:
CHRIS CURRY

Art Director:
CAROLINE MAILHOT

Publishing Company:
Condé Nast Publications, Inc.

Portrait of Nathanael West for "The Impostor", June 2, 1997, short story about the Paris art scene in the late 1920s.

Publication:
THE NEW YORKER

Illustration Director:
CHRIS CURRY

Art Director:
CAROLINE MAILHOT

Publishing Company:
Condé Nast Publications, In

GARY PANTER

118 Prospect Park West #5
Brooklyn, NY 11215
718-782-5420

Portrait of Eddie Vedder, lead singer of Pearl Jam, for the artic "The Courtship of Eddie Vedder" February 1998.

Publication:
DETAILS

Design Director:
ROBERT NEWMAN

Designer:
ALDEN WALLACE

Publishing Company:
Condé Nast Publications, In

Portrait of rap artist Puffy for th 'Cue' cover, December 1, 1997.

Publication:
NEW YORK MAGAZINE

Design Director:
MARK MICHAELSON

Art Director:
ANTON IOVKHNOVETS

Publishing Company:
Primedia, Inc.

BERTO **PARADA**
Levy Creative Management, LLC
East 46th Street #4G
York, NY 10017
-687-6463

290

stration entitled 'Cupid',
he feature "Esky",
ruary 1998.

lication:
QUIRE

ign Director:
BERT PRIEST

Director:
CKWELL HARWOOD

tor:
ER GRIFFIN

lishing Company:
Hearst Corporation

.F. **PAYNE**
Richard Solomon
Madison Avenue
York, NY 10013
-683-1362

291

sident Clinton, the first
mocratic President since F.D.R.
ave a second Inaugural; as
meth Starr prepares his
estigation, January 27, 1997.

blication:
ME

t Directors:
THUR HOCHSTEIN AND
NNETH SMITH

signer:
NNETH SMITH

itor:
ALTER ISAACSON

blishing Company:
ne Inc.

292

*The aged cast of TVs 'Seinfeld'
for "An Obsessive-Compulsive
Viewer's Guide to All 148
Episodes", May 30, 1997.*

Publication:
ENTERTAINMENT
WEEKLY

Design Director:
JOHN KORPICS

Art Director:
JOE KIMBERLING

Designer:
JOE KIMBERLING

Publishing Company:
Time Inc.

293

*Illustration for "Lincoln's Affair
of Honor", February 1998, a
story about a duel with the
Illinois politician James Shields.*

Publication:
THE ATLANTIC
MONTHLY

Art Director:
JUDY GARLAN

Publishing Company:
The Altantic Monthly

ALAIN PILON
6807 Drolet
Montréal, Quebéc
H2S 1T2 Canada
514-278-4090

294

*Movie poster for the film
'Le Siege de L'ame'.*

Client:
BEHAVIOUR
DISTRIBUTION

Art Director:
LOUISE LA FERRIÉRE

Designer:
DANIEL PROVENÇAL

Marketing Director:
JOHANNE PELLETIER

Design Firm:
Behaviour Design

295

*Illustration for "Ask the Spin
Doctors", July 1997, an article
on how to cool feet while cycling.*

Publication:
BICYCLING

Art Director:
JAMES VAN FLETEREN

Editor:
LISA GOSSELIN

Publishing Company:
Rodale Press, Inc

296

*Portrait of Harlem education
activist (and numbers racketeer)
Bumpy Johnson, for the feature "The
King and I", November 16, 1997.*

Publication:
THE PHILADELPHIA
INQUIRER MAGAZINE

Art Director:
CHRISTINE DUNLEAVY

Assistant Art Director:
SUSAN SYRNICK

Editor:
AVERY ROME

Publishing Company:
Philadelphia Newspapers, Inc.

297

*Portrait of Mathieu Kassovitz in
the movie 'A Self-Made Hero', for
the "Goings on About Town"
section, September 15, 1997.*

Publication:
THE NEW YORKER

Associate Illustration Editor:
OWEN PHILLIPS

Publishing Company:
Condé Nast Publications, Inc.

HANOCH **PIVEN**
c/o Sally Heflin & The Artworks
455 West 23rd Street #8D
New York, NY 10011
212-366-1893

298

*Portrait of Rosie O'Donnell, one
from a series for a story on food
and celebrities, February 1998.*

Publication:
SELF

Art Director:
KAYO DER SARKISSIAN

Publishing Company:
Weider Publications

299

*Portrait of Theodore Kaczynski,
the convicted Unabomber, as the
trial to determine his guilt and
sanity began, January 12, 1998.*

Publication:
TIME

Art Director:
KENNETH SMITH

Publishing Company:
Time Inc.

DAVID **PLUNKERT**
c/o Spur
3647 Falls Road
Baltimore, MD 21211
410-235-7803

300-301

*Illustration for "Taxpayers
Taxpower", January 1998,
an article on how to deal
with the IRS.*

Publication:
MONEY

Art Director:
RUDY HOGLUND

Designer:
HOLGER WINDFUHR

Editors:
ERIC GELMAN AND
WALTER UPDEGRAVE

Publishing Company:
Time Inc.

ARCHER **PREWITT**
1723 West Julian #2R
Chicago, IL 60622
312-862-4220

302

*Illustration for a paper promotion.
Copyline: "If you gaze for long
into the abyss, the abyss also
gazes into you".*

Client:
MOHAWK PAPER MILLS

Art Director:
DANA LYTLE

Designers:
BEN HIRBY
AND DANA LYTLE

Design Firm:
Planet Design

303

*Cover illustration for the feature
"Psychology of Back Pain",
Fall 1997.*

Publication:
STANFORD MEDICINE
MAGAZINE

Art Director:
DAVID ARMARIO

Editor:
LAUREL JOYCE

Publishing Company:
Stanford University
Medical Center

304

*Selected drawings from the
story "Sof'Boy", Fall 1997.*

Publication:
BLAB! #9

Art Director:
MONTE BEAUCHAMP

Designer:
MONTE BEAUCHAMP

Editor:
MONTE BEAUCHAMP

Publishing Company:
Fantagraphics

DEMETRIOS **PSILLOS**
17F Clerkenwell Road
EC1M 5RD London, U.K.

305

*Portrait of Rowan Atkinson for a
review of his movie 'Mr. Bean',
November 24, 1997.*

Publication:
THE NEW YORKER

Illustration Editor:
CHRIS CURRY

Publishing Company:
Condé Nast Publications, Inc.

CHRIS **PYLE**
135 North Wallace Avenue
Indianapolis, IN 46201
317-357-6015

306

*Illustration for the article
"Standing Room Only – And
That's Not Good", May 1997.*

Publication:
CONTINENTAL
MAGAZINE

Art Director:
JOHN HALL

Designer:
JOHN HALL

Editor:
TONY BOGAR

Publishing Company:
Cadmus Custom Publishing

LIZ PYLE
29 London Fields East Side
E8 3SA London, U.K.

307

The 'silver boy' with his 'silver cat', one from a children's book.

Publication:
SOMEWHERE OUT THERE

Art Director:
CAROLINE ROBERTS

Editor:
CAROLINE ROBERTS

Publishing Company:
Hutchinson's Children's
Books/Random House

ANDY RASH
298 Metropolitan Avenue #B4
Brooklyn, NY 11211
718-486-7820

308

*Unpublished portrait
of actor Tim Robbins.*

JOHN RITTER
228 Kingsbury Drive
Aptos, CA 95003

309

*One from a personal series which
explores the trafficking of young
women in Eastern Europe.*

VICTORIA ROBERTS
c/o Riley Illustration
155 West 15th Street #4C
New York, NY 10011
212-989-8770

310

*Personal piece entitled 'String
Theory of the Universe'.*

EDEL RODRIGUEZ
16 Ridgewood Avenue, Box 102
Mt. Tabor, NJ 07878
973-983-7776

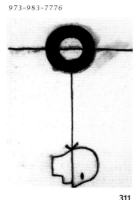

311

Untitled personal piece.

312

*Illustration for "The Plague
Years", January 26, 1998, a
memoir of Jon Lee Anderson's life
in Havana, Cuba*

Publication:
THE NEW YORKER

Illustration Editor:
CHRIS CURRY

Publishing Company:
Condé Nast Publications, Inc.

IRENE ROFHEART-PIGOTT
P.O. Box 420
Garrison, NY 10524
914-424-8304

313

*Illustration for the article
"Mother's Day – A Guilt-Edged
Occasion", May 11, 1997.*

Publication:
THE BOSTON GLOBE

Art Director:
RENA SOKOLOW

Publishing Company:
The Boston Globe

JONATHON ROSEN
612 Degraw Street #2
Brooklyn, NY 11217
718-855-6599

314

*Illustration of the movie 'Crash'
directed by David Cronenberg,
September 1997, for the "Home
Guide" video section.*

Publication:
PREMIERE

Art Director:
DAVID MATT

Designer:
BETHANNE NIEDZ

Editor:
SIMON BRENNAN

Publishing Company:
Hachette Filipacchi

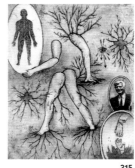

315

*Illustration for "The Prince of
Pain", Fall 1997, a tribute to the
late research psychologist and
humanist John Liebesking.*

Publication:
UCLA MAGAZINE

Art Director:
CHARLES HESS

Designers:
DANA BARTON AND
JACKIE MORROW

Editor:
JEFFREY HIRSCH

Publishing Company:
UCLA

316

*Series of key frames from the
CD-ROM 'Debauchery'.*

Client:
INSCAPE

Art Director:
REBEKAH BEHRENDT

Director:
JONATHON ROSEN

Animator:
AMY SHELTRAN

MARK RYDEN
541 Ramona Avenue
Sierra Madre, CA 91024
626-355-1750

317

*Portrait of singer Björk for
"Bohemian Rhapsody",
October 16, 1997, a review of her
album 'Homogenic'.*

Publication:
ROLLING STONE

Art Director:
FRED WOODWARD

Deputy Art Director:
GAIL ANDERSON

Publishing Company:
Wenner Media, Inc.

318

*Illustration for the story "Life in
the Air Ocean", November 1997.*

Publication:
GQ

Art Director:
JOHN BOYER

Editor:
ILENA SILVERMAN

Publishing Company:
Condé Nast Publications, Inc.

319

*Commercial pitchmen for the
feature "The Pauses That
Refreshed", March 28, 1997, a
list of the 50 best ads of all time.*

Publication:
ENTERTAINMENT
WEEKLY

Design Director:
JOHN KORPICS

Art Director:
JOE KIMBERLING

Publishing Company:
Time Inc.

320-321

*Personal piece entitled
'The Meat Magi'.*

JOSEPH SALINA
2255 B. Queen Street East #32
Toronto, Ontario
M4E 1G3 Canada
416-699-4859

*Illustration for "Cults –
The Next Wave",
February 1998, an article on
society's vulnerability to cults.*

Publication:
HOMEMAKERS

Art Director:
TRACY JOHN

Editor:
SALLY ARMSTRONG

Publishing Company:
Telemedia Communications In

MARK SAVAGE
444 Sackett Street
Brooklyn, NY 11231
718-624-5435

*Portrait of Harrison Ford for
"Hail to the Chief", July 28
1997, a review of the movie 'Air
Force One'.*

Publication:
THE NEW YORKER

Illustration Editor:
CHRIS CURRY

Publishing Company:
Condé Nast Publications, In

GERALD SCARFE
c/o I.C.M.
Oxford House
76 Oxford Street
W1N 0AX London, U.K.

*Unpublished portrait entitled
'J.F.K. and Friends'.*

Publication:
THE NEW YORKER

Illustration Editor:
CHRIS CURRY

Publishing Company:
Condé Nast Publications, In

ARD SCHUMAKER
Green Street
Francisco, CA 94133
-398-1060

325

entine's Day cover
tration featuring the perils of
ance, February 1998.
lication:
N FRANCISCO
AMINER SUNDAY
AGAZINE
Director:
Y RIGGS
or:
JL WILNER
lishing Company:
Francisco Examiner

ICHAEL SCHWAB
Tamalpais Avenue
Anselmo, CA 94960

326

-promotional portrait, also
ted for a paper promotion.
ent:
RINGHILL
Director:
Y RILEY
signer:
CHAEL SCHWAB
sign Firm:
chael Schwab Studio
ency:
den Marketing & Design

ARA L.
CHWARTZ
o West 67th Street #22G
w York, NY 10023
2-877-4162

327

ustration featured on apparel
the designer Anna Sui.

J.J. SEDELMAIER
c/o J.J. Sedelmaier Productions, Inc.
199 Main Street
White Plains, NY 10601-3200
914-949-7979

328

One of six key frames from the
video 'Larry the Luger'.
Client:
SLIMJIM-GOODMARK
Art Director:
STEVE GARBETT
Designer:
J.J. SEDELMAIER
Animator:
TOM WARBURTON
Producers:
JACK BLANDFORD AND
J.J. SEDELMAIER
Agency:
Northcastle & Partners

J. OTTO SEIBOLD
1261 Howard Street #3
San Francisco, CA 94103

329

"Ho-Ho-Ho", one from a
children's book, November 1997.
Publication:
OLIVE, THE OTHER
REINDEER
Art Director:
VIVIAN WALSH
Editor:
VICTORIA ROCK
Publishing Company:
Chronicle Books

LEANNE SHAPTON
R.R. #3
Caledon, Ontario
LoN 1Co Canada
519-927-3966

330

Unpublished idea
for a book cover.

331

Illustration for "The World He
Left Behind Him", June 14, 1997,
a review of Bruce McCall's
book 'Thin Ice: Coming of
Age in Canada'.
Publication:
THE GLOBE AND MAIL
Art Director:
GUDRUN GALLO
Editor:
MARTIN LEVIN
Publishing Company:
Thompson Newspapers

332

Four from a series of CD covers
for 'The Jazz Essentials' collection.
Client:
VERVE/POLYGRAM
(CANADA)
Art Director:
DAVID ANDOFF
Designer:
JUDY SETO

CHRIS SHARP
156 Ludlow Street
New York, NY 10002
212-505-0649

333

Illustration for a review of the
book 'Underworld' by Don DeLillo.
Publication:
GQ
Art Director:
JOHN BOYER
Publishing Company:
Condé Nast Publications, Inc.

DAVID K SHELDON
www.dksheldon.com
606-356-8203

334

David Grohl and the Foo
Fighters for a review of their
album 'The Colour and the
Shape', May 29, 1997.
Publication:
ROLLING STONE
Art Director:
FRED WOODWARD
Publishing Company:
Wenner Media, Inc.

WHITNEY
SHERMAN
5101 Whiteford Avenue
Baltimore, MD 21212
410-435-2095

335

One from a series entitled
'Cupids' Disguise', created for the
artist's website, 1997.

A. SKWISH
2436 Bush Street #2
San Francisco, CA 94115

336

Illustration for "Gunning for
Tarantino", November 9, 1997,
which asked: "Can Quentin
Tarantino live up to expectations?"
Publication:
CHICAGO TRIBUNE
Art Director:
THERESE SCHECTER
Designer:
STEVE RAVENSCRAFT

OWEN SMITH
1608 Fernside Boulevard
Alameda, CA 94501
510-865-1911

337

Cover illustration entitled 'The
Elephant Prophecy', for the
'Fiction Issue', June 23-30, 1997.
Publication:
THE NEW YORKER
Art Editor:
FRANÇOISE MOULY
Publishing Company:
Condé Nast Publications, Inc.

338

Portrait of actor Ving Rhames for
"Ving and a Prayer", September
5, 1997, a review of 'Rosewood'.
Publication:
ENTERTAINMENT
WEEKLY
Design Director:
JOHN KORPICS
Designer:
GEORGE McCALMAN
Publishing Company:
Time Inc.

339

Hunter S. Thompson, June 12,
1997, as his book of letters 'The
Proud Highway' is published.
Publication:
ROLLING STONE
Art Director:
FRED WOODWARD
Publishing Company:
Wenner Media, Inc.

EDWARD SOREL
156 Franklin Street
New York, NY 10013
212-966-3949

340-341

Caricatures from the movie
'Double Indemnity', for the article
"Vive le Noir", December 1997.
Publication:
GQ
Art Director:
KAY SPEAR GIBSON
Designer:
EDWARD SOREL
Editor:
ART COOPER
Publishing Company:
Condé Nast Publications, Inc.

MARCOS
SORENSEN
3531 25th Street
San Francisco, CA 94110
415-282-5796

342

Illustration for the article
"Spanish Guts – Waste Not,
Want Not", December 1997.
Publication:
AXCESS MAGAZINE
Art Director:
KARL OMELAY
Publishing Company:
Madhouse Media

JOE SORREN
P.O. Box 386
Lake Geneva, WI 53147-0386
520-214-9980

Illustration for the poem "Feather Shirt and Branches" by Motley, for the "Art Page", August 1997.
Publication:
SNOWBOARDER
Art Directors:
JAMIE MUELHOUSEN AND DOUG PALLADINI
Designer:
JAMIE MUELHOUSEN
Editor:
MARK SULLIVAN
Publishing Company:
Surfer Publications

Illustration for the poem "Lilly Anne and the Fish Parade" by Motley, for the article "Laundry Cafe", November 1997.
Publication:
WIG
Art Director:
DAWN KISH
Designer:
DAWN KISH
Editor:
KATHLEEN GASPERINI

GREG SPALENKA
21303 San Miguel Street
Woodland Hills, CA 91364

345

Illustration for the "The Last Act", November 1997, an article that reported on the rising number of teen suicides in Wisconsin.
Publication:
MILWAUKEE MAGAZINE
Art Director:
SHARON K. NELSON
Editor:
JOHN FENNELL
Publishing Company:
Quad Creative

RALPH STEADMAN
c/o Sobel Weber
146 East 19th Street
New York, NY 10003

346

Opening illustration for "Must Bleed TV", January 24, 1997, an article on the violence found in cable programming.
Publication:
ENTERTAINMENT WEEKLY
Design Director:
JOHN KORPICS
Publishing Company:
Time Inc.

347

Illustration for "Doomed Love at the Taco Stand", November 10, 1997, a report by Hunter S. Thompson from the set of 'Fear and Loathing in Las Vegas'.
Publication:
TIME
Art Directors:
ARTHUR HOCHSTEIN AND KRISTIN FITZPATRICK
Designer:
KRISTIN FITZPATRICK
Editor:
WALTER ISAACSON
Publishing Company:
Time Inc.

JAMES STEINBERG
115 Montague Road
Amherst, MA 01002
413-549-1932

348

Untitled personal piece.

349

Illustration for the article "Director 6 – Multimedia Studio", September 1997.
Publication:
MACWORLD
Art Director:
SYLVIA CHEVRIER
Editor:
KATE ULRICH
Publishing Company:
Macworld Communications

DUGALD STERMER
600 The Embarcadero #204
San Francisco, CA 94107
415-777-0110

350

One illustration from the upcoming book 'Visage'.
Designer:
DUGALD STERMER
Publishing Company:
Common Place Books

DONALD SULTAN
45 White Street #5
New York, NY 10013
212-343-2576

351

Opening illustration for the article "When Paris Comes Home", August 1997.
Publication:
TRAVEL & LEISURE
Design Director:
PAMELA BERRY
Designer:
DAN JOSEPHS
Publishing Company:
American Express Publishing

WARD SUTTON
799 Greenwich Street #4S
New York, NY 10014
212-924-4992

352

Illustration for "Blitzkrieg Pop", August 7, 1997, a review of 'The Fat of the Land' by Prodigy.
Publication:
ROLLING STONE
Art Director:
FRED WOODWARD
Publishing Company:
Wenner Media, Inc.

353

Illustration for a Broadway show poster.
Client:
FREAK
Art Director:
DREW HODGES
Designer:
KEVIN BRAINARD
Design Firm:
Spot Design

353

Illustration for the article "Peace is Hell", for the special 'Hollywood Issue', November 16, 1997.
Publication:
THE NEW YORK TIMES MAGAZINE
Art Director:
JANET FROELICH
Designer:
CATHERINE GILMORE-BARNES
Publishing Company:
The New York Times Co.

ELVIS SWIFT
817 Westwood Drive South
Minneapolis, MN 55416
Rep: Joanie Bernstein

354

Self-promotional piece.
Art Director:
ROBBIN TERRA

HIROSHI TANABE
c/o Kate Larkworthy Artist Representation, Ltd.
32 Downing Street #4D
New York, NY 10014
212-633-1310

353

illustration of the group Salt-N-Pepa for the article "The Original Spice Girls", December 1997.
Publication:
DETAILS
Design Director:
ROBERT NEWMAN
Designer:
ALDEN WALLACE
Publishing Company:
Condé Nast Publications, I...

Jack Palance and Brigitte Bar... for the revival of 'Contempt'.
Publication:
THE NEW YORKER
Associate Art Editor:
OWEN PHILLIPS
Publishing Company:
Condé Nast Publications, I...

AMY TANNER
P.O. Box B525
Annap... MN 20701
410-409-8999

One from a series for the article "Never Too Young: Developing Spiritual Values in Our Children", April 1998.
Publication:
JUBILEE
Art Director:
CATHERINE ELLIOT AZZAM...
Designer:
CATHERINE ELLIOT AZZAM...
Editor:
CARLA E. WILLIAMS
Publishing Company:
Alliance Media, Inc.

ARY TAXALI

. Box 272, Station C
nto, Ontario
N 2V7 Canada
-388-1334

358

onal piece entitled
bid the Sleuth'.

GREG TUCKER
1915 Lakeview SW
Albuquerque, NM 87105
505-873-3727

362

Illustration for the article
"Catholic is Not Enough",
May/June 1997.

Publication:
ENVOY

Art Director:
KINSEY CARUTH

Designers:
SUZY CARUTH,
LETITIA MONTOYA AND
BEN SNELL

Editor:
PATRICK MADRID

Publishing Company:
Envoy Publications

ARK TODD AND
THER WATSON

ndividual listings

359

al commissioned for the
York office reception area.

nt:
EDEN & KENNEDY

Directors:
RY KOEPKE AND
CY WALL

igners:
RK TODD AND
HER WATSON

ARK TODD

Prospect Place #1
oklyn, NY 11217
-783-1488

360

sonal piece entitled 'The
tory of the Cliffhanger'.

361

titled personal piece.

365

Illustration entitled "Future
of Technology", for the feature
"The Last Bit", July 1997.

Publication:
WORTH

Art Director:
PHIL BRATTER

Designer:
DEANNA LOWE

Editor:
JOHN KOTEN

Publishing Company:
Capital Publishing

JONATHAN
TWINGLEY
New York City
212-613-0906

363

One from a group of drawings
entitled 'The Ballad of William
Stover'. Here, God tells William
he is to sell bibles door-to-door.

MARK ULRIKSEN
841 Shrader Street
San Francisco, CA 94117
415-387-0170
Rep: Sally Heflin & The Artworks
212-366-1893

364

Illustration of Scottie Pippin
for a television ad.

Client:
WIEDEN & KENNEDY

Producer:
BETH HARDING

368

One of two from a series for
an investigation on the remaining
estate of slain rapper Tupak
Shakur, July 7, 1997.

Publication:
THE NEW YORKER

Illustration Editor:
CHRIS CURRY

Publishing Company:
Condé Nast Publications, Inc.

JACK UNRUH
2706 Fairmount
Dallas, TX 75201

366

Portrait of Julia Child for a
review of her autobiography,
October 13, 1997.

Publication:
THE NEW YORKER

Illustration Editor:
CHRIS CURRY

Publishing Company:
Condé Nast Publications, Inc.

369

One illustration from a series
for the article "Bites of Passage",
July/August 1997.

Publication:
SAVEUR

Art Director:
JILL ARMUS

Designer:
JILL ARMUS

Editor:
COLMAN ANDREWS

Publishing Company:
Meigher Communications

CHRIS VAN DUSEN
37 Pearl Street
Camden, ME 04843
207-236-2961

370

Self-promotional piece
entitled 'Girlfriend'.

367

Illustration for a fiction piece
entitled "P.S.", April 1997.

Publication:
GQ

Art Director:
JOHN BOYER

Editor:
ILENA SILVERMAN

Publishing Company:
Condé Nast Publications, Inc.

RICCARDO
VECCHIO
1 Christopher Street #12G
New York, NY 10014
212-647-9390

371

Cover illustration for the
feature "Casanova Was a Busy
Man", November 23, 1997.

Publication:
THE NEW YORK TIMES
BOOK REVIEW

Art Director:
STEVEN HELLER

Editor:
JONATHAN KEATES

Publishing Company:
The New York Times Co.

372

Opening illustration for the fiction
piece "Hollywood Shakedown",
November 1997.

Publication:
GQ

Art Director:
JOHN BOYER

Publishing Company:
Condé Nast Publications, Inc.

373

Portrait of Michael Tilson
Thomas for the feature "Go West
– Michael Tilson Thomas Gives
San Francisco a Symphonic
High", November 17, 1997.

Publication:
THE NEW YORKER

Illustration Editor:
CHRIS CURRY

Publishing Company:
Condé Nast Publications, Inc.

MAURICE
VELLEKOOP
c/o Reactor Art & Design, Ltd.
51 Camden Street
Toronto, Ontario
M5V 1V2 Canada
416-703-1913

374

One from a series for the fashion
story "Short Haul for the
Holidays", December 1997.

Publication:
WALLPAPER

Art Director:
HERBERT WINKLER

Designer:
ARIEL CHILDS

Editor:
TYLER BRUCE

Publishing Company:
Time Inc.

375

Cover illustration. One in a
series from a homoerotic 'primer'.

Publication:
MAURICE VELLEKOOP'S
ABC BOOK – A
HOMOEROTIC PRIMER

Designer:
MICHAEL ECONOMY

Editor:
KATHARINE GATES

Publishing Company:
Gates of Heck

ANDREA VENTURA
346 Leonard Street #2
Brooklyn, NY 11211

376

Portrait of Yohn O'Hara.
Publication:
THE NEW YORKER
Illustration Editor:
CHRIS CURRY
Publishing Company:
Condé Nast Publications, Inc.

376

Portrait of Pier Paolo Pasolini.
Publication:
THE NEW YORKER
Illustration Editor:
CHRIS CURRY
Publishing Company:
Condé Nast Publications, Inc.

JAMES VICTORE
64 Grand Street
New York, NY 10013
212-925-6862

377

Poster for a safe sex campaign.
Client:
DDD GALLERY
Art Director:
KOICHI YANO
Designer:
JAMES VICTORE
Design Firm:
James Victore Inc.

STEFANO VITALE
c/o Lindgren and Smith
250 West 57th Street
New York, NY 10107
212-397-7330

378

Illustration entitled 'Mother Memories', for a group of essays on Mothers, February 1998.
Publication:
LATINA MAGAZINE
Art Director:
LAURA ENCINAS
Editor:
PATRICIA DUARTE
Publishing Company:
Latina Publications

379

Illustration announcing a festival celebrating the centennial of Bram Stoker's 'Dracula', for the "Cue" cover, March 24, 1997.
Publication:
NEW YORK MAGAZINE
Design Director:
ROBERT NEWMAN
Designer:
PINO IMPASTATO
Editor:
CAROLINE MILLER
Publishing Company:
Primedia, Inc.

CYNTHIA VON BUHLER
16 Ashford Street
Boston, MA 02134
617-783-2421

380

Illustration for the article entitled "Prophecy", December 1997, describing a Hindu prophecy of doom and destruction.
Publication:
U.S. NEWS & WORLD REPORT
Art Director:
MICHELLE CHU

CHRIS WARE
Acme Novelty Library
1112 North Hoyne Avenue
Chicago, IL 60622

381

Selected drawings from the story "Tales of Tomorrow", Fall 1997.
Publication:
BLAB! #9
Art Director:
MONTE BEAUCHAMP
Designer:
MONTE BEAUCHAMP
Editor:
MONTE BEAUCHAMP
Publishing Company:
Fantagraphics

CHIP WASS
180 Varick Street 8th Floor
New York, NY 10014
212-741-2550

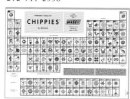

382

Promotional poster and reference chart for a dingbat typeface.
Client:
CHIPPIES BY WASSCO
Art Directors:
SCOTT STOWELL AND CHIP WASS
Designer:
SCOTT STOWELL
Design Firm:
Open
Agency:
Wassco

ESTHER WATSON
123 Prospect Place #1
Brooklyn, NY 11217
718-783-1488

383

Personal piece.

PHILIPPE WEISBECKER
c/o Riley Illustration
155 West 15th Street
New York, NY 10011
212-989-8770

384

One from a series for "Gap-Osis" August 25, 1997, an essay on economic inequality.
Publication:
FORBES
Art Director:
ROGER ZAPKE
Designer:
ROGER ZAPKE
Publishing Company:
Forbes, Inc.

384

Illustration for the article "In a Fishbowl".
Publication:
THE ATLANTIC MONTHLY
Art Director:
JUDY GARLAN
Designer:
ROBIN GILMORE-BARNES
Editor:
CULLEN MURPHY
Publishing Company:
The Atlantic Monthly

385

One from a series for "Big Blue – What Else Can You Do?", an article on nuclear testing, Fall 1997.
Publication:
THINK LEADERSHIP
Art Director:
STEPHEN DOYLE
Designer:
NAOMI MIZUSAKI
Editor:
PETER LEACH
Publishing Company:
IBM

LEIGH WELLS
250 West 22nd Street #4D
New York, NY 10011
212-627-8518

386

Illustration for a book about a women who discovers she has healing powers, and as a result, forms many interesting relationships – one with her grandmother who was a "turtle-woman" in a side show.
Publication:
THE HEALING
Art Director:
SARA EISENMAN
Designer:
LEIGH WELLS
Editor:
HELENE ATWAN
Publishing Company:
Beacon Press

MICHAEL WERTZ
385 1/2 Jersey Street
San Francisco, CA 94114
415-824-5542

Illustration depicting the opera 'La Traviata', for 'Three Faces of Love", July 1997.
Publication:
DIABLO ARTS
Art Director:
RENATE WOODBURY
Publishing Company:
Diablo Publications

ERIC WHITE
1142 Castro Street
San Francisco, CA 94114
415-821-3839

Personal piece entitled 'Critical Path'.

Concert poster for the Residents at the Fillmore Auditorium.
Client:
BILL GRAHAM PRESENT
Art Directors:
ERIC WHITE AND ARLENE OSEICHICK

ARAH **W**ILKINS
Riley Illustration
West 15th Street
York, NY 10011
-989-8770

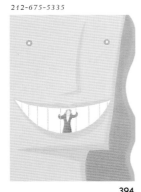

390

onal piece.

OMAS
OODRUFF
Cornelia Street #17
York, NY 10014
-924-4192

391

stration for "Alice's
nders", September 5, 1997,
view of Alice Hoffman's book
e on Earth'.

lication:
TERTAINMENT
EKLY

ign Director:
HN KORPICS

igner:
k BARNETT

lishing Company:
e Inc.

OAH **W**OODS
Westbourne Drive
Angeles, CA 90069
-659-0259

392-393

k cover for a paper
notion entitled 'Proterra'.

ent:
ORGIA PACIFIC
PERS

Director:
BESSER

igner:
BESSER

sign Group:
ser Design Group

D A N **Y**A C C A R I N O
95 Horatio Street Ste. 204
New York, NY 10014
212-675-5335

394

Personal piece entitled
'The Rage Inside'.

395

Illustration for "Love & Limits",
October 1997, an article on
teaching children how to behave.

Publication
PARENTING

Art Director:
SUSAN DAZZO

Designer:
BERNICE PFLUGER

Editor:
JANET CHAN

Publishing Company:
Time Inc.

M A R K **Z**I N G A R E L L I
1211 Reed Street
North Huntington, PA
724-861-8405

396

Illustration for the article
"The Next Thinker: Marx",
October 22-27, 1997

Publication:
THE NEW YORKER

Illustration Editor:
CHRIS CURRY

Publishing Company:
Condé Nast Publications, Inc.

B O B **Z**O E L L
2323 East Olympic #1
Los Angeles, CA 90021
213-629-0156

397

Index title page illustration.

L L O Y D **Z**I F F
Lloyd Ziff Design Group, Inc.
161 Henry Street
Brooklyn, NY 11201
718-855-7005

Creative Direction and Design.

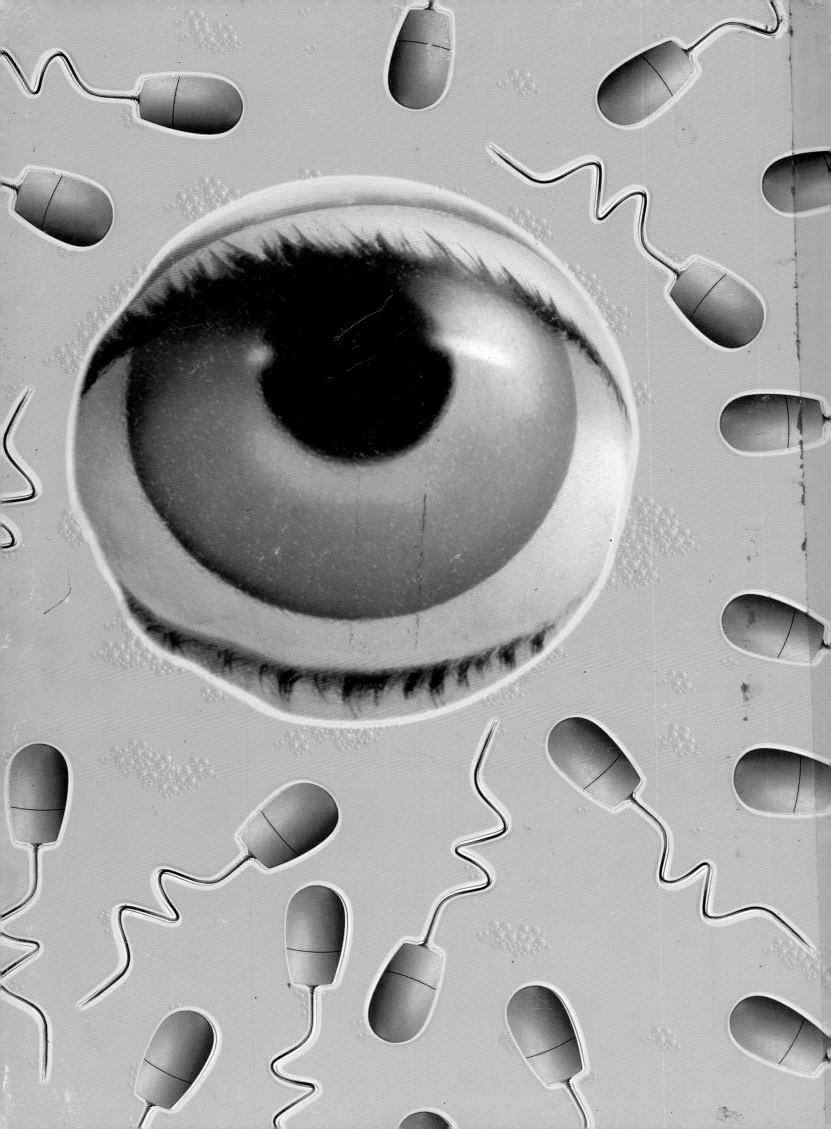